T0145874

ON-PLOT SANITATION

IN LOW-INCOME URBAN COMMUNITIES

Guidelines for Selection

ON-PLOT SANITATION
IN LOW-INCOME URBAN COMMUNITIES

Guidelines for selection

Andrew Cotton and Darren Saywell

Water, Engineering and Development Centre
Loughborough University
1998

Water, Engineering and Development Centre,
Loughborough University,
Leicestershire, LE11 3TU, UK

© Water, Engineering and Development Centre Loughborough University 1998

ISBN 13 Paperback: 978 0 90605 555 7
ISBN Ebook: 9781788533102
Book DOI: http://dx.doi.org/10.3362/9781788533102

A catalogue record for this book is available from the British Library.

WEDC (The Water, Engineering and Development Centre) at Loughborough University in the UK is one of the world's leading institutions concerned with education, training, research and consultancy for the planning, provision and management of physical infrastructure for development in low- and middleincome countries.

This edition is reprinted and distributed by Practical Action Publishing.
Since 1974, Practical Action Publishing has published and disseminated books and information in support of international development work throughout the world. Practical Action Publishing trades only in support of its parent charity objectives and any profits are covenanted back to Practical Action (Charity Reg. No. 247257, Group VAT Registration No. 880 9924 76).

Contents

Part 1

Part 2

Tables

Figures

Case studies

Field insight

Photographs

Glossary

Aqua privies
Latrine in which excreta fall directly through a submerged pipe into a watertight settling chamber below the floor, and from which effluent overflows to a soakaway or drain.

Arithmetic mean
The sum of the values of all observations divided by the number of observations.

BOD
Biochemical oxygen demand: the mass of oxygen consumed by organic matter during aerobic decomposition under standard conditions, usually measured in milligrams per litre during five days; a measure of the concentration of sewage.

Excreta
Faeces and urine.

Compost latrine
In this type of latrine, excreta fall into a watertight tank to which ash or vegetable matter is added.

Dry latrine
A latrine where users defecate into a bucket, basket or other receptacle that is regularly emptied. This type of latrine forms part of the nightsoil system.

Latrine
Place or building, not normally within a house or other building, for deposition, retention and sometimes decomposition of excreta.

Overhung latrine
Latrine sited such that excreta falls directly into the sea or other body of water.

Median
The value above which and below which half of the cases fall, the 50th percentile.

Mode
The most frequently occurring value (or values).

Nightsoil
Human excreta, with or without anal cleaning material, which are deposited in a bucket or other receptacle for manual removal (often taking place at night).

Off-set pit
Pit that is partially or wholly displaced from its superstructure.

On-plot sanitation
Sanitation systems which are contained with the plot occupied by the dwelling. On-plot sanitation is associated with household latrines, but also includes facilities shared by several households living together on the same plot.

On-site sanitation
Includes communal facilities which are self-contained within the site, in contrast to sewerage and dry latrines where excreta is removed from the site.

Pathogens
Organism that causes disease.

Percolation rate
The rate at which liquids move through soil.

Pit latrine
Latrine with a pit for accumulation and decomposition of excreta and from which liquid infiltrates into the surrounding soil.

Pour-flush latrine
Latrine with a small quantity of water is poured in to flush excreta through a water seal into a pit.

Sanitation
The means of collecting and disposing of excreta and community liquid waste in a hygienic way so as not to endanger the health of individuals or the community as a whole.

Septic tanks
Watertight chamber for the retention, partial treatment, and discharge for further treatment, of sewage.

Sewage
Wastewater that usually includes excreta and that is, will be, or has been carried in a sewer.

Sewer
Pipe or conduit through which sewage is carried.

Sewerage
System of interconnected sewers.

Soakaway
Soakpit or drainage trench for subsoil dispersion of liquid waste.

Soakpits
Hole dug in the ground serving as a soakaway.

Sullage
Wastewater from bathing, laundry, preparation of food, cooking and other personal and domestic activities that does not contain excreta.

Superstructure
Screen or building of a latrine above the floor that provides privacy and protection for users.

TACH
Total annual cost per household; includes capital (or investment) costs and recurrent costs.

Vent pipe
Pipe provided to facilitate the escape of gases from a latrine or septic tank.

VIP latrine
Ventilated improved pit latrine, pit latrine with a screened vent pipe and a partially dark interior to the superstructure.

Water seal
Water held in a U-shaped pipe or hemispherical bowl connecting a pan to a pipe, channel or pit to prevent the escape of gases and insects from the sewer or pit.

Wastewater
Sewage or sullage.

Y-junction
Chamber in which liquid may be directed along either of two pipes or channels.

Part 1

Section 1A
Background

Section 1B
Guidance points in relation to latrine type

Section 1C
Guidelines for key questions

Section 1D
Cross cutting issues

Section 1E
Conclusions

Section 1A:
Background

Project details

This document presents the findings from Phase 2 (August 1994-March 1997) of Project R4857 *On-Plot Sanitation in Low Income Urban Communities* carried out by the authors as part of the Technology, Development and Research Programme, Engineering Division, Department For International Development of the British Government. The project concerns the performance of on-plot sanitation systems in India, Ghana and Mozambique.

Purpose

Phase 1 (a comprehensive literature review) found there was little clear evidence of an objective examination of the performance and sustainability of on-plot sanitation in urban areas of less developed countries. The purpose of Phase 2 is to investigate how satisfactory on-plot sanitation is in the urban context, and to develop guidance on its use for policy makers and professional staff of urban governments, development agencies and non-government organisations.

Background

The Phase 1 review recorded an underlying feeling amongst some authorities and sector professionals that whilst on-plot sanitation was appropriate for rural areas, it was generally unsuitable in the urban context, unless viewed as a (preferably short-term) route to 'better' forms of sanitation. Given the reality of the situation in which on-plot sanitation is widespread in urban areas, this project seeks to investigate some of the key issues of concern through field investigations in India (Vijayawada), Mozambique (Maputo) and Ghana (Accra, Cape Coast and Tamale).

The most important feature of our investigation is that it focuses on the *perceptions* of the users of on-plot sanitation (see the outline methodology). All too often, assessments and judgements on the effectiveness and appropri-

3

ateness are made from a technologically biased and purely external perspective. One can observe that many evaluations are done by those who are hardly likely to themselves be regular users of improved pit latrines. We have therefore devoted most attention on an attempt to establish what the concerns of the users of on-plot systems were in urban areas and to reflect these in the guidance offered.

About these Guidelines

The results of our investigations are presented in this document as a series of *guidelines* for selection and use of on-plot sanitation. It *does not intend to give those who use it a formula with which to make decisions* - it is primarily a means for **narrowing** decision making at the local level.

The Phase 1 report identified a number of important issues which have guided this investigation; these are reflected in our findings which are presented in the following way. In **Section B**, we briefly describe the different on-plot technologies, offer guidance on situations in which the particular technologies are appropriate, and present the users' perceptions as a series key findings for:

- Unimproved pit latrines
- Lid-covered pit latrines
- Ventilated improved pit latrines
- Double pit pour-flush latrines
- Pour-flush toilet to septic tank
- Bucket/pan latrines

In **Section C**, we pose five key questions which emerged during the Phase 1 review and postal survey in relation to the use of on-plot sanitation in urban areas. We provide specific guidelines and supporting evidence in relation to each of these key questions, which include:

- What are the reasons for the absence of household sanitation?
- Will users be satisfied with on-plot solutions to sanitation?
- How does plot size constrain the use of on-plot sanitation?
- What operational problems arise with on-plot sanitation?
- Do maintenance problems arise when pits and tanks fill up?

In **Section D**, we abstract four important cross-cutting issues which emerged during the course of the investigation and provide guidelines on each. In fact,

4

these issues are common to the development of any sanitation programme whether on-plot or off-plot, but we deal with them as best we can from the perspective of on-plot sanitation programmes:

*   Role of socio-cultural factors in user choice
*   Cost, subsidies and cost recovery
*   Institutional considerations
*   Promotion of sanitation

Section E presents our conclusions.

The scope and focus of this project is related to *user perceptions* of on-plot technologies. We would like to reinforce the point that factors relating to the development of successful *sanitation programmes*, particularly institutional and promotional issues, need additional detailed investigation. A new DFID project (R6875), now underway, entitled *Practical Development of Strategic Sanitation Approaches* will redress these deficiencies.

Methodology

The research employed several different methodological tools simultaneously, some of which were conducted in-country, others from the United Kingdom. Ghana, Mozambique and India were selected for fieldwork visits on the basis that these countries would afford cross-cultural and technological comparisons. Arrangements were reached with several agencies (NGO's, government departments, municipalities) to collaborate on the research and to provide the necessary in-country inputs of resources to conduct appropriate fieldwork.

Household surveys
House to house surveys formed the basis of the data output. In each country, local field workers, known by the communities in which they worked, were employed to collect data using a locally agreed questionnaire survey sheet. The selection of districts to be surveyed was left to the discretion of collaborating agencies, but general criteria included:

*   Districts in which collaborating agencies had a history of community based work
*   Districts with mixed physical site conditions
*   Districts with mixed density housing

5

- Districts with varying household plot sizes
- A mixture of formally and informally developed areas
- Areas where pit emptying practices could be found and observed

A total of 1843 completed household surveys were conducted during this stage of the research.

Semi-structured interviews
Semi structured interviews involve a series of open-ended questions that are asked in a largely predetermined order. Each question is followed with additional probes until an answer is explored in some depth. A total of 15 interviews with staff from implementing agencies, multilateral agencies, government ministries and NGO's were used to build up qualitative data relating primarily to programme and some technical related issues.

Quantitative testing
Tests for numbers of flies contained with latrine superstructures were conducted on 73 household latrines and 2 public latrines. Testing involved leaving adhesive 'fly' paper in latrine superstructures for a standard test period to sample for flies. Categories of flies were noted and checked against a guide sheet. Planned tests for odour and wind flow across vent pipes proved inconclusive and were subsequently abandoned.

Postal surveys
Surveys of engineers, administrators, health workers, and government officials were conducted by post. The questionnaire focused on similar issues to the household survey but required the respondent to give an overview for his/her city. 58 completed postal survey questionnaires were used in the research, a response rate of 19% .

Literature review
An on-going literature review covered both general issues and those relating in particular to groundwater pollution.

6

Section 1B:
Guidance points in relation to latrine type

Latrine types

This section briefly reviews some of the most commonly encountered on-plot sanitation systems and presents specific findings in relation to each of them. The systems included are:

- Unimproved pit latrines
- Lid-covered pit latrines
- Ventilated improved pit latrines
- Double pit pour flush latrines
- Pour-flush toilet to septic tank
- Bucket/pan latrines

Detailed descriptions of these have been well documented elsewhere (See for example: Cotton & Franceys (1991), Franceys, Pickford & Reed (1992)).

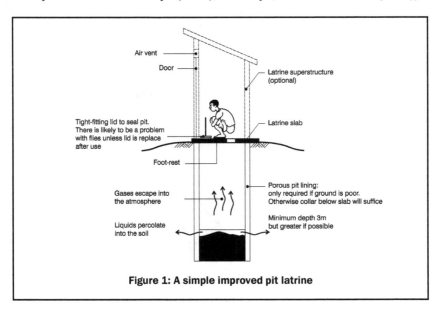

Figure 1: A simple improved pit latrine

The principle underlying all types of pit latrines is that excreta and anal cleansing material can be deposited in a hole in the ground. Its basic components are a superstructure to provide user privacy, a hole or seat set into a slab which covers the pit, and a pit beneath the slab into which excreta is deposited.

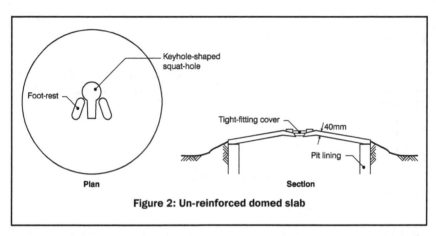

Figure 2: Un-reinforced domed slab

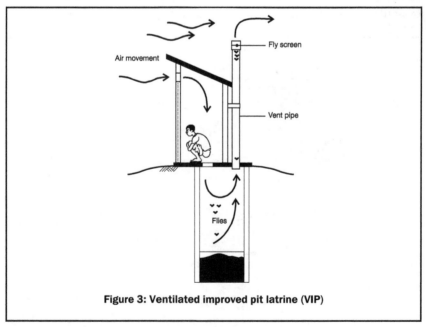

Figure 3: Ventilated improved pit latrine (VIP)

The addition of a lid which fits tightly into the hole in the slab should help to reduce insect and odour nuisance.

The important feature in the Ventilated Improved Pit Latrine (VIP) is the addition of a vent pipe whose purpose is to reduce the escape of odour and insects through a squat hole by creating a through-flow of air. The vent pipe needs to extend about 300mm above flat or sloping roofs or the apex of conical roofs to benefit from a draught passing across the pipe. Flyproof netting is fixed across the top of the vent.

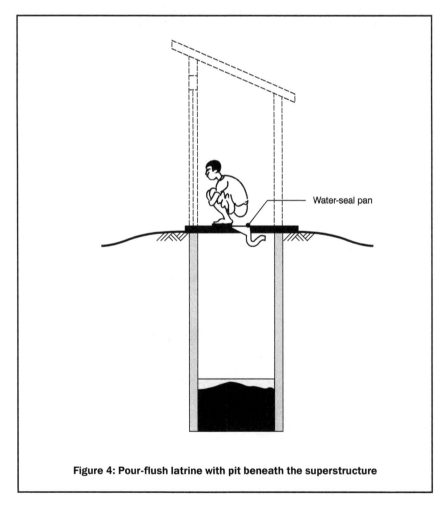

Water-seal pan

Figure 4: Pour-flush latrine with pit beneath the superstructure

Latrines with water seals are suitable where water is used for anal cleaning. The pour-flush latrine has a bowl inserted into the hole in the slab; when filled with water this creates a seal which isolates the pit from the superstructure and the user, thereby both improving the aesthetics of the latrine and reducing insect and odour nuisance. With a well designed, smooth surface pan only one or two litres of water are required for cleaning. There are several variants of the pour-flush latrine depending on the location and number of pits in relation to the latrine superstructure and pour-flush slab. The pit can either be below the slab, or offset from it and connected via a short length of pipe to a sewer. In the latter case, a further option is to provide two shallow pits which are used/emptied alternately; we refer to this as the double pit pour-flush latrine.

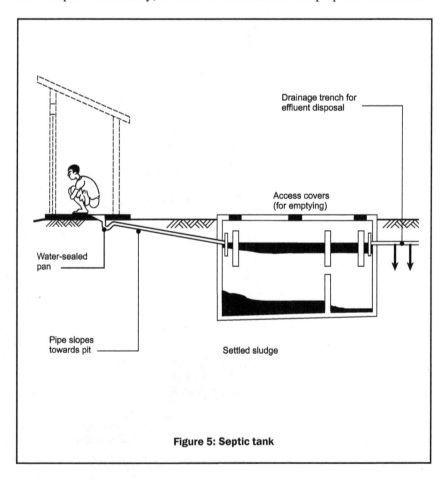

Figure 5: Septic tank

A septic tank is an underground watertight settling chamber into which sewage is delivered through a building sewer connecting a cistern flush toilet to the tank. The sewage receives partial treatment in the tank; effluent infiltrates from the tank into the surrounding ground through soakage pits or trenches.

Bucket or pan latrines involve a container made of (non-corrosive) material which is placed beneath a squatting slab or seat in a chamber, with rear doors which are kept shut except during removal and replacement of the bucket.

Guidance points in latrine selection

It is not possible to prescribe precise routes for selecting a particular type of on-plot latrine, because it is always difficult to allow for local contextual factors which influence the type of latrine householders obtain. For example, an important but unstated assumption of most decision algorithms (particularly those with a technological bent) is that consumers have a completely free choice over the range of options. This is not necessarily the case, for example, where programmes choose to promote or subsidise particular technologies. Another situation which defies the rather technocratic approach of deducing the best type of latrine via a series of checklists is where there exists social pressure to acquire a latrine built to a certain design and specification.

We therefore suggest the following selected *guidance points,* which are based on the findings of our survey of user perceptions of the particular technology. These points will provide the reader with detailed information about specific technology types, and should be used to gain a better indication of the problems which might arise when advocating these types and the conditions in which their use might be appropriate. Alongside these points we present selected illustrative caselets.

Cost to the householder is the overwhelmingly important factor; different types of latrine clearly have different costs, added to which subsidies may be available for certain target groups to use a particular design of latrine. There is also a trade off between capital and operation & maintenance costs in relation to the size of the pit. Deep pits, whilst more expensive to construct, have a longer life-cycle and therefore incur less cost with regard to pit emptying. This applies to all types of pit latrine with the possible exception of double pits systems which are usually constructed because there is an express reason for requiring shallow rather than deep pits.

The simple improved pit latrine is the lowest cost option (see **GP1**).

At marginally increased cost, the hole in the latrine slab can be sealed by a tight fitting lid, which in theory reduces insect and odour nuisance (see **GP2**).

Ventilation of the latrine pit also has been advocated as a means of reducing fly and insect nuisance; this adds to the cost of the latrine, being more expensive than providing a sealed lid (see **GP3**).

If water is used for anal cleansing, it is possible to use a pour-flush latrine. We were only able to investigate the double pit pour-flush latrine, and have no detailed information on either single pit direct or single pit offset latrines which did not exist in substantial numbers in the study areas. The addition of the pour flush bowl and connecting sewer add significantly to the cost (see **GP4**).

If a plot has an individual piped water connection supply, a cistern flush toilet may be used which is connected to a septic tank. This option has the highest construction, operation and maintenance costs of all of the on-plot options studied (see **GP5**).

Finally, we also looked at the cases of households served by bucket latrines. The generally unhygienic and hazardous operation of this system means that in common with other authorities we would not recommend that this system be adopted anywhere. Bucket or pan latrines are amongst the oldest forms of organised sanitation, and are still used extensively throughout the cities and towns of Africa, Asia and Latin America. Although the number of bucket latrines are declining rapidly, this type of system remains attractive because of its low capital cost. The normal format for this system involves a container made of (non-corrosive) material which is placed beneath a squatting slab or seat in a chamber, with rear doors which are kept shut except during removal and replacement of the bucket (see **GP6**).

Unimproved simple pit latrine: selected guidance points (GP1)

Based on 39 cases (2% of full sample): Mozambique 60%, Ghana 40%.

- 66% level of overall user satisfaction

- User satisfaction levels most significantly affected by smell and smell and insects

- 80% of users felt the problems they had identified had no or slight impact on its use. Users perceived lower cost (39%) and easier operation and maintenance as ways to alleviate identified problems with their latrine

- Insect and odour nuisance were relatively high. 51% recorded a 'strong' smell from their latrine, 25% recorded 'hundreds' of flies

- Mean construction cost: Ghana (US$ 26), Mozambique (US$ 9)

- 24% of all latrines had been in use for more than 5 years

- The majority of pit latrines (84%) had not been emptied. When they had, most were on one occasion only. 58% of all cases recorded re-emptying periods greater than 3 years

---

Lid-covered latrine: selected guidance points (GP2)

Based on 357 cases (19% of full sample): Mozambique 92%, Ghana 8%.

- Few cases of problems with simple pit latrines recorded, reinforced by a 93% level of overall user satisfaction

- Most significant problems affecting user satisfaction were smell and insects (8% of respondents) and frequent repairs (6%)

- 25% of all simple pit latrines had been in use for more than five years

- Only 6% of pit latrines been emptied, most on one occasion only. Re-emptying periods were greater than three years in most cases; only 1% of the sample regarded pit emptying as an operational problem

NB: In Mozambique the convention for latrine superstructures is a privacy screen with no roof. It was observed that this aided reduction of odour and insect nuisance since there was no containment of foul smells or flies within the superstructure.

Ventilated Improved Pit (VIP) latrines: selected guidance points (GP3)

52 cases (3% of full sample) all drawn from Ghana.

- 83% level of overall user satisfaction expressed

- User satisfaction levels are most significantly affected by smell, insects and emptying problems

- 61% of users believed that the problems they had identified with their latrines had no impact on its use. Users perceived easier operation and maintenance and less regular need for emptying (9%), and lower cost (36%) as ways to alleviate identified problems

- 10% of users recorded high incidences of insect nuisance, and 60% noted slight or strong smells

- Mean construction cost 313,000 cedis (US$156), mean emptying cost, 30,000 cedis (US$15)

- 42% of VIP latrines required emptying every six months, with 53% being emptied by vacuum tanker

- 33% of VIP latrines had been in use for more than five years

- 46% of all latrines had not been emptied; 6% of these had been in use for more than 5 years

---

Pour-flush latrine: selected guidance points (GP4)

394 cases (21% of full sample) all drawn from India.

- 83% level of overall user satisfaction expressed

- User satisfaction levels are most significantly affected by smell, blockage and frequent repairs

- 69% believed that the problems were minor and of little impact; of the remainder, users perceived these problems could be alleviated by easier operation and maintenance and less regular emptying (60%), and lower cost (27%)

- 5% of users recorded moderate incidences of insect nuisance, and 36% noted slight or strong smells

- Mean construction cost Rs2866 (US$78), mean monthly O&M cost Rs33 (US$0.9)

- For 59% of all latrines, the period between being emptied exceeded three years. In 27% of cases, this period lasted for five years or more

...GP4 continued

- Pour flush latrines have been constructed on plots as small as 14m^2
- 62% of pour flush latrines had been in use for more than five years
- 66% of all latrines had not been emptied; of these, 47% had been in use for between 6-10 years

Case study 1a: Pit emptying of pour-flush latrines

District:	*Pakeer gudem*
City:	*Vijayawada, India*
Family size:	*10; (5 adults - 5 children)*
Income earners:	*1*
Occupation:	*Mason*

Notes: Resident in this slum for 20 years, the family had constructed a low cost sanitation toilet in 1987/88 (a pour flush twin pit system of 6ft depth in each pit); prior to this the family had used public latrines. The household were given instructions and a demonstration on use of the latrine at the time of construction. In conversation with the family, it was clear that they knew and understood that when 'water did not flow' it was necessary to alternate pit use. The pits had been emptied only once and municipal 'scavengers' had been contacted for this purpose. Emptying took two nights work, cost Rs 400 (US$ 11) for both pits, and was completed by hand using buckets, hand tools and a handcart. The pit contents were disposed of off-site (in a designated place to receive faecal matter). The householders reported that the contents of the first pit was hard and black on sight, indicating it had been rested for its specified 'safe' period.

Case study 1b: Pit emptying of pour-flush latrines

District:	*Bhinana Vari Peta*
City:	*Vijayawada, India*
Family size:	*8; (5 adults -3 children)*
Income earners:	*1*
Occupation:	*Milk project worker*

Notes: This pour-flush twin pit system had been in use for seven years with eight users, and had been emptied twice (with a three year re-emptying period). Scavengers were employed to empty the pits, at a cost of Rs 800 (US$22) per pit (this figure was higher than normal due to the difficult local terrain). The hilly nature of the slum meant that a cart and drum could not be positioned next to the plot for emptying, as in the normal manner. Thus, pit contents were diluted with water prior to emptying and removed by hand with buckets. The contents were dumped into lane-side drains which were then flushed with water. These drains were later 'disinfected' by the scavengers (although no details of how this was done were given). The householder did not report any significant problems with the latrine other than with emptying, which the householder felt was expensive and was inconvenient to neighbours.

...GP4 continued

Field insight 1: Experiences with pour-flush double pit latrines

Case:	*1*
District:	*Readhe Nagar*
City:	*Vijayawada, India*
Family size:	*3 adults, 1 child*
Income earners:	*2 (Rs. 60 per day, per person)*
Occupation:	*Agricultural labourer/coir production worker*

Notes: This family was using a pour flush twin pit system which had been incorrectly constructed with a connection *between* pits, instead of the normal Y-junction. The toilet had been used in this fashion for eight years, and because the pit required such frequent emptying, some members of the family had decided to resort to open defecation in order to reduce maintenance costs. This was considered highly unsatisfactory by the house-holders because of the lack of privacy afforded.

Case:	*2*
District:	*Fraizerpet*
City:	*Vijayawada, India*
Family size:	*5 adults, 7 children*
Income earners:	-
Occupation:	-

Notes: This family had been using the same latrine for the last 5 years (a pour-flush twin pit). The pits were alternated in 1995, and prior to this it had taken three years for a single pit to fill. In conversation with the householders, it became clear that they were aware of how to alternate the pits (demonstrating how to block the Y-junction, and being able to identify the signs of a full pit), and that the twin pit system was designed to facilitate and improve the pit emptying process.

The household did not report any problems with the operation and maintenance of their latrine. They had applied for a latrine under the programme because it would provide 'comfort and convenience' (the family had resorted to open defecation prior to using this system). No significant odour problem or insect nuisance was reported. Where insects nuisance was noted, the householders believed its source was primarily from lane side drains, not the latrine itself. Plot size estimated at 112m².

Case:	*3*
District:	*Ranader Nagar*
Family size:	*6 adults, 2 children (2 families)*
Income earners:	*4 (Rs. 100 per week)*
Occupation:	*Metal workers*

Notes: Two adults from this family had stopped using the latrine because they preferred open defecation. The pour-flush twin pit system had been in use for 1.5 years without

...GP4 continued

any need for emptying. At the time of the completion of the latrine, no instructions or demonstration had been given to the householders on how to use the latrine or what to do when one pit became full. The family had applied to build a latrine under the existing sanitation programme because of (a) the lack of privacy with open defecation, and (b) the flooding of the Krishna river reduced places for open defecation during the rainy season.

Despite the lack of support, the family reported that they were highly satisfied with the operation and maintenance of their latrine. Mosquitoes were a nuisance at night but the householders felt they were derived from the drain which was present at the back of the plot, not the toilet itself. Plot size 27m².

Case:	4
District:	Ranader Nagar
City:	Vijayawada, India
Family size:	4 adults, 1 child
Income earners:	1 (Rs. 600 pcm)
Occupation:	Labourer

Notes: This family had used their latrine for a total of eighteen months. Some members of the family continued with open defecation outside of the rainy season. When the latrine was first constructed, the users were given a demonstration by the masons as to how to operate and maintain the toilet, including the correct operation of the Y-junction.

The family had experienced problems with blockages (thought to be attributable to the high density plastic pans) though these were infrequent. They had decided to pay a 'scavenger' to clean and maintain the latrine each week (at a cost of Rs 2 per week).

The reason for applying for, and constructing the latrine, was the 'difficulty' of going to the banks of the Krishna to defecate ('difficulty' implying problems of convenience and privacy).

WC to septic tank: selected guidance points (GP5)

159 cases (9% of full sample); 82% from Ghana, 18% from India.

- 90% level of overall user satisfaction expressed

- User satisfaction levels most commonly affected by lack of water and tank emptying

- 86% believed that the problems were minor and of little impact; of the remainder, problems could be alleviated by easier operation and maintenance and less regular emptying (55%), more regular water supply (13%) and lower cost (10%)

- No significant incidences of insect nuisance, and 33% noted slight or strong smells

- Monthly O&M cost (US$0.3 - US$5)

- In 34% of cases, the period between emptying the tanks exceeded three years. 23% required emptying every six months

- 58% of all households had used septic tanks for more than three years. 36% of these had used the facility for more than 11 years

- 48% of septic tanks had not been emptied during their lifetime

Bucket/pan latrines: selected guidance points (GP6)
264 cases (14% of full sample) all drawn from Ghana.

- Only 33% overall user satisfaction expressed

- User satisfaction is most affected by the frequency and cost of emptying, associated smells and insect nuisance

- Of those who expressed problems, 84% believed that they had a significant impact; of the remainder, users felt problems could be alleviated by easier operation and maintenance and not requiring regular emptying (49%), simpler toilet design (26%) and lower cost (9%)

- 13% of users recorded high incidences of (flying) 'insect' nuisance and 60% presence of cockroaches. 90% noted slight or strong smells

- Mean construction cost (US$24), monthly O&M cost 5346 cedis (US$3)

- 25% of bucket/pan latrines have been in use for between 21-30 years

Case study 2: Bucket/pan latrine use

District:	*Nima*
City:	*Accra, Ghana*
Family size:	*30; (20 adults - 10 children)*
Income earners:	*15*
Occupation:	*Petty traders / drivers*
Consumer items:	*Television; radio*
Plot size:	*1120m²*

Notes: The motivating factors for these compound housing families to build a household toilet was primarily social: comfort & convenience and privacy. The decision to build a bucket/pan latrine instead of other toilet types was a function of the bucket/pan's low cost. The latrine had been constructed with the house in 1960 and was paid for at the time through the landlady's own financial resources. Amongst the range of problems identified about the latrine, 'smell' and 'emptying' were most significant. Emptying was undertaken every three days by a private contractor at a price of 800 cedis (US$ 0.4) per visit. The householders believed that the bucket's contents were disposed of hygienically off-site. Emptying was very irregular and this had led some of the household to resort to open defecation. In general, the household were 'satisfied' with their bucket latrine, but felt that the problem with flies, insects and emptying was significant enough to have a 'strong impact' and made its use 'a constant problem'. Easier operation and maintenance was seen as the key to relieving these difficulties.

Section 1C:
Guidelines for key questions

In this section we present five key questions which are central to the adoption of on-plot sanitation in urban areas and provide specific guidelines and supporting evidence in relation to each. For each key question, readers are referred to *Part 2: Supporting evidence* for a detailed explanation of these points.

Key Question 1

What are the reasons for the absence of household sanitation?

Guidelines

- Poverty and indebtedness are the primary reasons for lack of household latrines. When money is available, it may be prioritised for other essential items

- Householders decide to invest in domestic sanitation for socio-cultural rather than health reasons

---

Background
- Poverty, and/or the inability to save funds to invest in longer term sanitation facilities are key factors for absence of sanitation on-plot.
- Significant family indebtedness, often due to payment of medical fees through illness, constrain ability to save or invest in sanitation.
- In cases where plot size was mentioned as the key factor explaining absence, these cases were spread across a range of plot size categories, rather than being exclusively linked to the smallest size group.
- Plot sizes amongst households without sanitation are not on average smaller than those households where latrines are present.
- The relationship between cost, technology choice and income level is a complex one, which defies simple categorisation. There is some evidence to suggest grouping of unskilled employment with those households without sanitation, although this does not remain true for lower cost

latrine types. Similarly, skilled sources of employment are not the sole source of employment with higher cost latrine types. Choices about sanitary technology are based on a variety of factors, of which cost is just one (important) consideration.

Case study 3: Absence of household latrine: 1

District: *Ranigarathotha*
City: *Vijayawada, India*
Family size: *8; (4 adults - 4 children)*
Income earners: *1*
Occupation: *Ice cream vendor (Rs. 70 per day) during summer; vegetable vendor during winter*

Notes: Before moving to Ranigarathotha, this family had lived elsewhere in Vijayawada and had used a pour-flush twin pit latrine. Financial problems led them to sell their old plot in order to move to this district. On the current plot, they had used a pour-flush twin pit latrine between 1990-95, but due to the need to pay their daughter's medical fees when she fell ill, the family was forced to subdivide the plot and sell half to their neighbours. The sold portion contained the household latrine. All family members have subsequently resorted to open defecation, on grounds 200 metres from the house. This proved very inconvenient for the female head of household because of the lack of privacy from open defecation. The family wanted to build a new toilet under the slum improvement scheme next to their current bathroom; they felt that there was sufficient space on their plot to do so, and were confident that by saving they would be able to afford the repayment costs involved in construction. Plot size approximately 54m².

District: *Bhinana Vari Peta*
Family size: *2 adults; 4 children*
Income earners: *2 (Husband - Rs. 20-25 per day; son - not stated)*
Occupation: *Rickshaw puller (husband); agricultural labourer (son)*

Notes: The family moved to this district so that they could be closer to the fields they worked and in order to buy their own land. The family had resorted to open defecation both at their previous and current plots. Since moving to the hill slum nine years ago, defecation has involved walking approximately 1km to relieve themselves on open ground, a trip which involved ascending and descending steep stairways on each occasion. During conversation with the family, the main factor accounting for the absence of a household latrine was 'lack of money' (the family were indebted to the sum of Rs. 5000-6000 from medical fees incurred during a child's illness). Additionally, they lacked legal title to the land which had previously been a constraint, but this had recently been granted by the Municipality. Major expenditure items included subsistence spending on food and goods to sustain their livelihood(s), and their current loan liabilities.

Case study 4: Absence of household latrine: 2

District: *Readhe Nagar*
City: *Vijayawada, India*
Family size: *1*
Income earners: *1 (Rs. 20- per day; 600-700 pcm)*
Occupation: *Coir production worker*

Notes: The household consisted of a single woman who had moved to Vijayawada from elsewhere in Tamil Nadu twenty years previously. During the first 12 years at this site, there had been no household sanitation provision available. When a facility was built, it soon collapsed and since that time, the woman had resorted to open defecation. The householder had not used the toilet when it had been built on the plot because of operational problems ('the water did not flow'). She was not aware that there was a current low cost sanitation scheme at work in the slum, and expressed a desire to build a latrine if the government was prepared to help finance it. She reported that it was inconvenient to continue to defecate in the open because of the increased number of plots in the slum and the reduced number of (nearby) locations for open defecation (privacy problem). The majority of her income was spent on repaying the loan which was taken on buying the house; on the upkeep of livelihood as a coir production worker and on the flooring for the house (flagstones). The householder was currently unable to afford a share in the cost of a low cost toilet.

Key Question 2

Will users be satisfied with on-plot solutions to sanitation?

Guidelines
- Users express a high degree of satisfaction with on-plot sanitation
- In this survey, 83% to 90% were 'satisfied' or 'very satisfied'

Background
- For all latrine types other than bucket/pan latrine, users expressed high degrees of satisfaction with their latrine (in excess of 80% recording 'satisfied' or 'very satisfied'). Interestingly, simple improved pit latrines (assumed to be the most problematic of on-plot systems) recorded slightly higher levels of user satisfaction than VIPs or pour-flush latrines.
- Many users do not perceive there to be any problems with their latrines (accounting for 54% of the total sample). Where problems are recorded, the most common relate to the emptying of pits/tanks. However, in absolute terms, this figure is low (12% of total sample).
- Other problems, such as smell, insects and operational problems relating to the emptying of pits and tanks have the most impact on satisfaction levels and the ability for the householder to use the latrine. However, these figures still only account for 6% of the total sample.

Key Question 3

How does plot size constrain the use of on-plot sanitation?

Guideline
- Small plot size is not a constraint to the use of on-plot sanitation

Background
- Operational sanitation facilities were found to be commonplace on the smallest of plot sizes: 14m^2.

- Levels of user satisfaction were not significantly affected by the incidence of small plot size.
- There is little indication that plot size determines technology choice. No definitive grouping or concentration of technology types was observed by recorded size categories.
- There is little indication that plot size is associated with particular operational problems. Where the most common latrine problems were noted, they were spread across all size categories.
- The absence of household sanitation is not exclusive to the smallest plot sizes.

Key Question 4

What operational problems arise with on-plot sanitation?

Problem 1: Odour and insect nuisance

Guideline
- This problem is not extensive; very few users perceive odour and insect nuisance to be a common problem with their latrine

---

Background
- Only 11% of the total sample mention either odour (7%) or insects (4%) as a nuisance problem (although nuisance of this kind does have a significant impact on satisfaction levels).
- VIP latrines record higher than anticipated levels of odour and insect nuisance. There is little conclusive evidence to suggest a link between odour and insect nuisance and: height of vent pipe above roof line, presence of fly screens, vent pipe colour and diameter of pipe.
- Quantitative test results for insect nuisance indicate low absolute numbers of insects observed across a range of latrine types.
- Anecdotal evidence raises doubts about domestic latrines as the primary source of insect nuisance on the household plot.
- Bucket/pan latrines register the highest nuisance levels of all latrine types.

Case study 5: Source of insect nuisance on-plot

District:	*Mearuthi Nagar Canal Huttings*
City:	*Vijayawada, India*
Family size:	*2 adults, 3 children*
Income earners:	*1 (Rs. 4000 pcm)*
Occupation:	*Clerk, Medical college*

Notes: This household had been using a pour-flush latrine with a sewer connection since 1994. The latrine was built entirely from family resources, and the household expressed a high degree of satisfaction with their facility. The household head reported that the family felt that the main source of insect nuisance was that arising from the drains which ran adjacent to the household plot, not from latrine superstructure itself.

Problem 2: Incorrect operation of double pit latrines

Guideline
* Mechanisms needs to be in place for ensuring that correct operation is explained at both the planning and post-construction stages

Background
* Insufficient user support and education activities were made available to users.
* Construction related problems were infrequently noted by users. Of greater concern were correct operation and maintenance of twin and double pit latrines.

Problem 3: Groundwater pollution

Guidelines
* Pollution of groundwater constitutes a potential environmental hazard but not necessarily a health risk

* A minimum distance of 15 metres, other than in fractured formations, between a pit and a downstream water point is sufficient to remove contaminants

Background
- Determining the movement of viruses and bacteria in soils is extremely difficult, and involves a complex interaction of soil profile and hydraulic conductivity parameters, temperature, soil pH, and moisture retention capacity. The clay content of the unsaturated zone is amongst the single most important indicator of the likely mobility of contaminants and its subsequent impact on groundwater pollution.
- Larger sized contaminants (helminths and protozoa) are normally effectively removed by physical filtration; bacteria are normally filtered by clayey soils. Of most concern are waterborne viruses which are too small for even fine grained clays to filter.
- Viruses *normally* die-off within three metres of the pollution source, irrespective of soil type. Bacterial contamination is *normally* removed given sufficient depth of unsaturated soil (at least 2 metres) between the pollution source and water point.
- Health risks associated with environmental pollution of groundwater must be set against the much greater hazard of widespread open defecation and contamination of the neighbourhood environment with excreta.
- If a health risk is demonstrable, investigate alternative water supplies through extending reticulation systems as this is likely to be cheaper than centralised sewerage with treatment.

Key Question 5

Do maintenance problems arise when pits and tanks fill up?

Guidelines

- Advise householders that the filling/emptying cycle is likely to be between 3 to 6 years and that they need to make their own arrangements for desludging

- Emptying cost is strongly location specific; investigate likely emptying costs with local contractors during programme planning

---

Background
- Manual methods of emptying tend to dominate, and are especially commonplace for simple pit and pour-flush latrines. As expected, mechanical emptying tends to be associated with VIP and septic tank latrines.

27

- The responsibility for emptying latrines is normally either that of the users, or contractors. Contractors are of particular importance in the emptying of bucket/pan and pour flush latrines.
- For those latrines which had been emptied, most had been used for 6, 7, or 8 years. Typically, these latrines had been emptied either once or twice.
- Rates for re-filling of previously emptied latrines indicate that the majority fill over 3-6 years.
- Where users expressed a problem with emptying, the three most important issues were frequency, cost and hygiene.
- In the majority of cases, the final disposal site for collected excreta was either unknown or indiscriminate dumping.

Field Insight 2: Emptying pour-flush latrines by scavengers

District: *Scavengers' Colony*
City: *Vijayawada, India*
Occupation: *Pit emptiers*

Notes: 'Scavengers' (the local terms applied to individuals emptying pits) are generally self employed, although some do work as Municipal road sweepers. While some empty pits on a full time basis, others work as scavengers only part time. In order to qualify as a scavenger, an individual must apply for and be granted a collectors certificate by the Municipality and work in the same community for a minimum of six months. Indian scheduled caste status tends to constrain scavengers' ability to work in other forms of employment.

Scavengers hear about full pits which need emptying either by householders coming directly to the scavengers' communities or through their work as road sweepers. The average workload for a scavenger is one house every 10-15 days. It normally takes 3-4 hours to empty both pits, using buckets, water drums and transport using a rickshaw. On arriving at the household, the procedure is to open the slab cover, empty with buckets into drums and dispose of the contents away from the site. In hill terrain slums, scavengers were placing the pit contents in lane drains and flushing the contents to the ground level with water. Generally, pit contents are disposed of in major outfall pipes or on surrounding fields.

When asked about the condition of the excreta removed from pits, the scavengers did not have a common experience with regard to the texture and colour of pit contents. Some found that the faeces in both pits were fresh and soft (indicating incorrect operation), whilst others found the contents to be hard and innocuous (indicating adequate resting period). Costs for emptying were set at Rs 50 for each pit ring of each pit emptied (6 rings to a pit) though it was claimed that in hill slums charges for pit emptying could rise to as much as Rs 2000.

The overheads involved in emptying included rent for rickshaw and drums, but this tended to vary from case to case depending on the distance travelled to the plot. For a fee of Rs 300, overheads may account for between Rs 50-100. The remainder was split between the scavengers (normally three persons for each pit emptying).

Section 1D:
Cross-cutting issues

In this section, four important cross-cutting issues which emerged during the course of the investigation have been abstracted and guidelines on each are provided. In fact, these issues are common to the development of any sanitation programme whether on-plot or off-plot, but we deal with them as best we can from the perspective of on-plot sanitation programmes:

* Role of socio-cultural factors in user choice
* Costs, subsidies and cost recovery
* Institutional issues
* Promotion of sanitation

Socio-cultural issues

Guidelines

* In planning sanitation interventions, programme staff need to be sensitive to the social and cultural context in which decisions about sanitation facilities are made, if there is to be widespread adoption of the programme

* There is a potentially wide differential in understanding of key concepts about hygiene, health and sanitation between users and programme implementers. Interventions should seek to look at their activities from the user's perspectives, knowledge and understanding

* Communities are rarely uniform. Different groups have specific needs with regard to sanitation

* Different groups exercise different levels of authority over the community and act as a constraint or aid to promotion and change

* Individual users decide whether to accept or reject new sanitation facilities. Sanitation interventions depend on the consent of the individual - they need to be convinced of the need for the improvement and that any benefits will outweigh any costs

Background

Sanitation programmes involve much more than simply designing a particular engineering solution to fit a particular problem. As important as an appropriate technological option is an understanding of the social context and the complex relationship of beliefs, traditions and social structures which are common to a given community. By ensuring that any engineering intervention is acceptable to its intended user group(s), the chances of implementing a programme that is sustainable over the longer term are significantly increased. It is therefore necessary to understand at the design and planning stage of a sanitation intervention what the critical factors are which determine how a community operates.

Cultural beliefs

Attitudes and behaviours which are derived from a combination of tradition, religion, and moral standards can have a powerful influence on the use and acceptability of on-plot sanitation systems. Understanding what these influences are will help to inform the process of selecting technology and improve the acceptability of sanitation improvements. For example, culture may determine the technical parameters which are set for a given technology: the type of anal cleansing material used (typically determined by custom or tradition rather than notions of hygiene and health) will have implications for the technical design of a sanitation system.

Culturally derived ideas of what constitutes improper or taboo practices affects the use of sanitary facilities by particular social groups. In peri-urban Mozambique, it was reported that mother and sons-in-law should not use the same latrine (based around maintaining respect) and women were frequently forbidden from using a latrine during menstruation because the men of the household feared 'catching diseases'. Likewise, the need for privacy during defecation (particularly for women) is a critical factor affecting both the use of a latrine and the design of the superstructure.

Communities typically have well developed ideas about what constitutes hygiene, disease and sanitation. Concepts of dirty and clean will vary markedly between traditional and Western notions, and between programme promoters and users. Careful appreciation of these concepts are key elements in designing promotion campaigns in which users are encouraged to accept an intervention because of new standards of cleanliness. Judgements between those beliefs which are beneficial to improved sanitation, and those which are not needs to be made. An example of the effect of such concepts is that is many societies it is commonly and wrongly held that children's excreta is less harmful than that of adults. A study of nearly 8,000 individuals in India (GOI, 1990) showed that the general understanding was that unweaned infants' excreta was 'absolutely harmless' because it came from mother's milk.

Case study 6: Influence of belief systems on siting of household latrines

A slum area in Vijayawada, Andhra Pradesh, India had been upgraded but the community were not using the new toilets provided on their plot. This was not immediately apparent, but when a local woman resident was asked by a speaker of the local language if there had been any problems with the recent development, she explained that most of the households had not been using the toilets provided. She explained that the toilets were located in the north-east corner of the plot, and according to the Hindi belief system Vastu, this is an inauspicious place to locate a toilet. The north-east corner is preferential for items such as a water source, the prayer room and the main door. Toilets should be located at the south of the plot. As a result, many residents did not use the toilets provided, and had resorted to open defecation in fields adjacent to the slum.

Social structure
Communities are rarely homogenous, but are formed from a diverse number of ethnic, political, age and gender groups. Each of these groups will have specific roles and patterns of behaviour within a community which will affect their needs vis-à-vis sanitation. Consider for example the different needs that women and men have with regard to sanitation: with the former a high premium is placed on the need for privacy during defecation, and the inaccessibility of public latrines after dark are key concerns which are gender specific.

Key change agents
Communities often develop informal and indigenous organisational forms which have evolved over time to assist in the functioning and operation of a society (for example, chiefs, elders). These different groups exercise different levels of authority and power within a community and have the potential to influence community decision-making and the process of change in both a positive and negative manner. Identification of *who* the key change agents

are is a critical element for effective sanitation promotion and implementation. In the Kumasi Sanitation Project (KSP), Ghana, the role of area chiefs in the sanitation programme was of key importance. These chiefs acted as the main link between the metropolitan assembly and the community, and their overall task was to keep the community informed, develop a dialogue with the people and encourage participation in sanitation related activities.

"I have asked the communities to make an effort to construct latrines in their homes. I have also talked to them about the dangers of cholera, dysentery and other diseases that they will suffer if the sanitary conditions in the community is not improved. The people accepted the challenge; it was rather progressive. Initially, five people volunteered to have improved latrines constructed in their homes, then it increased to ten and so on. I have myself constructed a latrine in my house to serve as an example"

– Chief of Moshe Zongo, Kumasi, Ghana (UNDP-World Bank Water and Sanitation Programme: RWSG-WA, 1994)

Furthermore, understanding *why* certain groups are open or resistant to change helps to determine how promotional activities should be conducted and what strategy for implementation should be adopted. Change agents may be resistant to an intervention for various reasons, including factors such as resentment towards outsiders and experts and the fear of loss of authority over the community through community development programmes. An NGO working in Accra, Ghana on the implementation of a ventilated improved latrine programme in low income urban districts noted a series of problems with community 'assemblymen' (the representatives of the municipal assembly at the local level). Assemblymen had responsibility for promoting and developing sanitation programmes at the local level (in consultation with the community) and in this case were a focus of the repayment process. Semi-structured interviews showed that in some cases:

- Assemblymen would agree to policy decisions during sanitary committee meetings when implementing agencies were present, but the moment the NGO withdrew from the district, the assemblyman would change procedure and practices to suit their own agenda
- Money was collected from the community for repayment purposes (via the assemblymen) but not paid back into the revolving fund scheme

Costs, subsidies and cost recovery

Guidelines

- The views of sector professionals about the affordability to the user of a particular latrine type may be at variance to the householder's idea of what is and is not affordable

- Systems providing credit for financing sanitation generally involve a high management burden for programme staff

- Forms of social contracting such as peer pressure, peer guarantees and tribal court systems are effective methods of cost recovery compliance

- Schemes which accommodate periods of household financial stress have greater potential for sustainability

- Cost recovery schemes which redirect revenue back to the community for other development interventions could improve repayment schedules

- In rented accommodation, or other areas where there is insecurity of tenure, improvements to sanitation facilities may simply lead to higher rents, forcing the poorest to move out

---

Background

Although different sanitation interventions may exhibit a range of social, cultural, institutional, technical and health related features which make them more or less desirable for implementation, the choice of one option over another is frequently based on the cost of the technology and its affordability to potential beneficiaries. It should not be assumed that because a sanitation technology is marketed as being 'low(er)-cost', that low income urban households perceive it to be so, or can actually afford it. If they cannot pay, then the options are typically to either provide a subsidy, or to arrange for a loan.

The recent shift in development thinking away from supply-led financing strategies to those that are demand-based implies that if the financial element of a sanitation programme is to be sustainable, considerable information about the financial context in which communities operate will be required. This includes information relating to the availability of credit facilities, the willingness of the communities to pay for sanitation, government attitudes towards cost recovery, the role of the private sector and so on. Some of these aspects are considered below.

Costs

A feature of on-plot sanitation systems is that the majority of the costs are for local material or labour. Equipment and supplies imported from abroad may have a range of prices, from low 'official' rates to ten or twenty times as much on the open market. Similarly, official conversion rates between local and 'hard' currency may be unrealistic. The effect is that attempts to give an international cost to different types of sanitation are of very limited value. Subsequent costs in this section are only for in-country comparison and analysis.

The single most useful figure for comparing sanitation costs is the total annual cost per household (TACH). This includes capital (or investment) costs and recurrent costs adjusted to reflect real opportunity costs and averaged over time. Examples of calculating and using TACH and other methods of cost comparison for sanitation can be found in Franceys, Pickford and Reed (1992), and in the Annex.

Beyond methods of comparing costs, user perceptions of the relative affordability of a sanitation option are critical for programme sustainability. If costs are perceived to be too high by users, then householders will be unwilling to invest in sanitation. It is important to note that there can be large differentials between what professionals and beneficiaries accept as a 'low(er)' cost technology.

In Mozambique, the national low cost sanitation programme has introduced unreinforced domed concrete slabs, which are targeted at the poorest sections of peri-urban communities, who typically earn less than 217,000 Meticals (MT), (US$22) per month. The total cost of producing a simple slab in 1995 was 105,200 MT (US$10.99), and with subsidies from government and donor agencies, user contributions were reduced to 11,100 MT (US$1.16). Additional costs were borne by the users through transportation of slabs from production units, and from the construction of the latrine superstructure.

Household surveys asked users to describe the total cost of their latrine as 'low', 'medium', or 'high'. The table below indicates results for those latrines built most recently in 1995 or 1996.

The key point is that despite the subsidy provided, this relatively simple technology type was still perceived by large sections of users to be of 'medium' cost. This reinforces the difficulties of providing comparable

36

Table 1: User perceptions of simple pit latrine costs for facilities built in 1995 and 1996, Mozambique

Year	User perception of total cost of latrine (% of cases)		
	Low	Medium	High
1996	18	22	9
1995	16	28	8

sanitation costings - in many other parts of the globe, the total cost figure used here might be considered very low, but it is the local context and the particular demands that householders have on their income which complicates such comparisons.

Case study 7: Impact of 'high cost' KVIP's in Ghana

The high cost to the user of KVIP's in Ghana (where they were first introduced) has seriously impeded the implementation of urban sanitation programmes (Brown,1985). Although both the government and the Ghana Water and Sewerage Corporation have adopted the KVIP as the 'approved' type of on-plot sanitation there has been a comparatively low rate of construction because of high costs. In Kumasi, conversion costs from a bucket latrine to KVIP were 60 per cent of the cost of a new KVIP.

Affordability and types of financial assistance

There is a degree of consensus in existing literature that suggests a range of 1.5-3 per cent of total household income represents an 'affordable' level of financing for household sanitation facilities. Amongst the poorest sections of the community, this figure may fall to 1-1.5 per cent of total income.

Where the cost of a technology type exceeds this general range, then financial assistance of one form or another for construction of the facility will probably be necessary. All costs involved in operation and maintenance and future upgrading of the facility should be the responsibility of the user so as to ensure sustainability.

There are a variety of approaches to financial assistance which may be considered.

Subsidies and grants

If a sanitation intervention is to target the poorest urban communities, then some form of subsidy and/or grant has to be provided (Roy, 1984). The use of subsidies can lead to numerous problems, many of which have been well documented. Typically, these might include:

- Money is not directed at sanitation provision
- Subsidies may lead to the adoption of a technology type which is financially unaffordable which will ultimately bring problems with the future operation and maintenance of the facility
- Subsidies can bring with it unfortunate or undesirable perceptions or associations which can taint a technology type
- Means testing for subsidies may lead to richer members of a community misrepresenting their status in order to benefit from what is available
- Subsidies reduce the profit potential for private sector contractors to become involved in latrine construction
- Different subsidy levels are provided by different agencies and donor organisations

If subsidies are to be introduced then certain key elements need to be designed into the scheme (EHP, 1997).

- Conduct willingness to pay surveys prior to designing the programme. Different sections of the community will be prepared to pay differential rates for adequate sanitation
- Consider the full real cost of assisting the whole target population. Can this be met within the existing programme budget?
- Allow potential for upgrading to take place by providing subsidy for only the most basic facility
- Fund only the interventions which are likely to have the greatest health impact

Even with the poorest households, a nominal loan component is seen as an invaluable way in which to maintain household commitment to the programme and to ensure longer term operation and maintenance of the facility.

Loans

Loan schemes, whereby money is made available from the government or a donor agency at normal or subsidised interest rates and repaid over time, is an important financing measure and offers opportunities for involving the poorest sections of a community in a way that community self-financing may not. However, ensuring regular repayment of the loan is difficult, and numerous examples of failed credit schemes have been documented in the sector. EHP (1997) have identified some commonalities about the situations in which these schemes have failed:

• Financial environments in which inflation has been, or is, high
• Where it is not common to borrow money for capital goods
• Where unplanned demands on household finances mean that regular repayment is unlikely

Revolving funds are a specific type of loan scheme in which a limited fund of money is available for a particular programme, and it is incumbent on the beneficiary household(s) to repay their loan in order that other community members can access this fund. Peer pressure, peer guarantees or examples of social, rather than legal contracts for repayment, are increasingly important and effective methods of cost recovery. A good example of this form of social contracting is Operation Hunger's sanitation initiative in Kwa-Jobe, KwaZulu/Natal, South Africa. In this scheme, residents agreed to pay 44 per cent of the capital costs of household VIP latrines (roughly US$78) over a six month repayment period. The mechanism agreed on to ensure cost recovery was an existing tribal court system to 'discipline' those who failed to maintain repayment. Additionally, a staggered delivery system was used whereby funds and materials were only released for new applications once the sanitation committee could demonstrate reconciled accounts and that previous recipients had fully complied with the repayment schedule.

Lessons learnt for effective cost recovery include:

• Use of social rather than legal sanctions
• There is a need for transparency in loan repayment arrangements. Householders must be able to have access to and understand the status of a revolving fund. In Kumasi, Ghana, householders had no access to the repayment schedules used in the household sanitation component, and were suspicious of over-billing

39

- Repayments schedules need to recognise and accommodate periods of financial stress for householders
- Loans for latrines should have shorter repayment periods than for housing, since the perceived benefits of latrines are limited and may not sustain payments over a longer period
- Some form of commitment from the beneficiary (either in the form of a deposit or labour during construction) is desirable. If a programme does not capture participation from the community in this form, then low returns on loan schemes are probable
- Interviewing potential beneficiaries before granting loans may help to reduce defaulting. In Ouagadougou, Burkina Faso, beneficiaries under the Strategic Sanitation Plan were filtered according to their ability to make substantial savings

---

Case study 8: Experiences of cost recovery and one NGO's response

---

An Accra based NGO working in low income high density urban communities comment on their experiences of cost recovery with a domestic KVIP programme.

"Well, I think that considering the amount of income people earn and the amount you are expecting them to pay at the end of the month, you realise that somebody who is supposed to pay about 157,000 cedis (US$165) to cover the cost of a VIP latrine will be paying a monthly [repayment] fee of 6,000 cedis (US$6). Maybe his total income is about 40,000 cedis (per month) (US$42) - but from this they have to pay rent, have to pay for the family, for electricity, for water, so even 6,000 cedis was too much. A few times we would have to come in and get the money from the people, and...I have personally said on a few occasions to people who cannot pay the 6,000 cedis - 'What can you afford at the end of the month?', which means that the 24 months repayment becomes 36 months or something. So I personally tell them to pay less...far, far less - about 20 per cent less. I think we should have flexible repayment rates. Considering the areas in which we are working...if you are telling them to repay the money and the rate of repayment at the end of the month is far above what they can pay, that will be a nonsense. So the payments should be less, or there is a need for some flexibility".

Community self-financing

With this approach, no external funding is made available for sanitation improvements, instead the programme responds to expressed user demand and their willingness to pay. In areas with large proportions of rented accommodation, or in areas which do not have security of tenure, the potential for self-financing may be severely limited, since few tenants are willing to invest in improvements which ultimately benefit their landlord. Additionally, better facilities within rented accommodation may simply give way to higher rents, forcing the poorest to move away.

Institutional issues

Guidelines

- Maintain clear lines of responsibility between participating agencies in sanitation projects

- Effective co-ordination of different agencies may produce better conceived and more acceptable sanitation options for communities

---

It should be noted that factors relating to the development of successful sanitation programmes, particularly institutional and promotional issues, need additional detailed investigation. A new DFID project (R6875), now underway, entitled Practical Development of Strategic Sanitation Approaches will redress these deficiencies.

Background

Any sanitation intervention takes place against a background of complex relationships between different stakeholders, including the household, community, and government. The nature of these relationships inevitably affects the way in which a programme is planned, implemented and managed. Institutions or organisations which play a key part in this relationship include those bodies outside the local community which are responsible for initiating, promoting, supervising and supporting a sanitation intervention.

Institutional responsibility

Many institutions have a stake in sanitation in the urban context, from central government ministries, through local authorities, and non-governmental organisations. The provision of services to urban communities involves many providers working on connected tasks. In such an operating environment, problems such as poor co-ordination of programme activities, duplication of efforts, and institutional conflicts can arise, all of which weaken the attainment of the projects goals. A key factor in achieving and sustaining programme success is the creation of a clear institutional structure with a lead agency to take overall control of the intervention, to establish clear areas of responsibility, goals and objectives, and a time frame and schedule to achieve these goals. Designated officers and advisory committees working within the lead agency can make the task of executing the programme or project easier.

Case study 9: Institutional responsibilities under the SSP, Kumasi, Ghana

---

In Kumasi, Ghana, the Strategic Sanitation Plan (SSP) brought about significant changes to the existing institutional arrangements in order to introduce greater transparency and clarity to infrastructure provision in the city. Prior to the SSP, the management of sanitation services and the institutional roles of the Kumasi Metropolitan Authority were fragmentary and unclear. The Medical Officer of Health, Mechanical Engineer's Department and the Metropolitan Engineer's Department were jointly responsible for planning, development, operation and maintenance of household sanitation, public latrines and solid waste collection and disposal. The division of responsibilities between the three were fraught with duplications and inefficiencies. Following implementation of the Plan, the KMA were stripped of responsibility for direct delivery of waste management services, and instead wide partnerships between the communities and private sector were encouraged. An independent waste management department (WMD) was created to oversee this transition and to plan and supervise waste collection and disposal undertaken by different participating agencies. The department was headed by a Director of Waste Management who was directly accountable to the metropolitan chief executive via the director of administration. Furthermore, clear division of responsibilities was brought about through the creation of four sections within the WMD: contract management, administration, pollution control and planning.

Institutional co-ordination and cooperation

Identifying a lead agency does not mean that an intersectoral approach cannot be pursued. Other organisations have specialist skills and knowledge which would prove invaluable in deciding which technology to apply and how to implement such a programme. Discussions with key informants during this research indicated that cross sectoral co-ordination and cooperation was frequently lacking or poorly developed in programmes. To achieve a greater degree of dialogue between key sector agencies, a series of components to reinforce partnership arrangements were identified:

- Specialised teams or working groups to deliberate on specific issues of relevance (i.e., sanitary codes and regulations)
- Steering committees comprising representatives from the range of cross sectoral institutions working on a particular intervention (see case study 10 below)
- Regular meetings and reports circulated to all partners
- A formalised contractual arrangement outlining the responsibilities of all partners

However, establishing *effective* dialogue and cooperation between sector agencies remain the critical issue. The points listed above will only work if all participating agencies are committed to working together.

Case study 10: Urban Sanitation Improvement Team, Ghana

In Accra, Ghana, the Waste Management Department for the city wanted to introduce a programme of construction of domestic KVIP latrines in low-income districts. At the executive level, an Urban Sanitation Improvement Team was established with the intention of bringing together representatives from the planning department, the Ministry of Health, the Ministry of Public Works as well as the Waste Management Department to co-ordinate activities and inputs from the respective agencies.

The key lessons which had been learnt from the creation of such specialised teams was that they need to be given a clear remit, their role in existing organisational structures needs to be clarified and their staff should be given designated duties, rather than incorporating team activities within existing workloads.

Such specialised teams frequently offer opportunities to overcome the bureaucratic procedures and delays which can beset the institutional aspects of sanitation interventions.

Lead agencies must decide how most effectively to use the experience of multilateral and NGO support for sanitation programmes, and to try and incorporate their efforts appropriately into the overall scheme. Tendencies for NGO's to promote one-off projects which fulfil their own objectives can be damaging to the overall programme goals. In Mozambique, the National Low Cost Sanitation Programme had found that the reputation of their programme had to some extent suffered through poorly developed and ill-advised NGO sanitation interventions which failed soon after implementation. The Programme has begun the process of lobbying central government to issue guidelines to NGO's which will allow wider monitoring of their work programmes.

Institutional - householder roles: catalysts
When a project is implemented, it is valuable for the implementing agency to have contacts with the community, as a means for stimulating participation, assessing need and co-ordinating implementation. For example, in Mozambique, local community members, or animators, are used by the national programme to promote the programme in the local area, help assess the individual needs of those without sanitation, to monitor and evaluate the performance of the system and to reinforce hygiene behaviour practices.

Particular elements of the community may be more effective in communicating messages than others. For instance, women have a special role in running the home, collecting water and managing the sanitation system, thus, female animators, or talking to female heads of households about sanitation are important elements.

Field insight 3: Institutional framework to National Low Cost Sanitation Programme (PNSBC), Mozambique

---

Operational organisation
This is structured around a single central management unit located in the capital, Maputo, and a series of improved latrine projects (PLM's) at the provincial level.

Responsibilities

The Programme is managed nationally by a central management unit (CMU) which has responsibility for overall policy, planning, co-ordination, training, resource mobilisation, procurement and financial management. The CMU maintains supervisory visits to each of the provincial units as a means of ensuring quality control in the programme: each unit is expected to be visited at least once every two months. There are currently 8 Improved Latrine Projects (PLM's) at provincial level. Each unit has responsibility for planning, budgeting and projecting annual production targets.

Institutional framework

The PNSBC emerged out of the initiatives of the National Directorate of Housing and National Directorate for Preventative Medicine in the 1970's. It was subsequently absorbed into the Institute of Physical Planning (INPF) which was a suitable institutional location at the time given the complementary roles with urban and rural contexts. Since the dismantling of the INPF and the creation of the Institute of Rural Development, there have been concerns about the logic of the institutional framework.

The water supply and sanitation sector as a whole in Mozambique has suffered from institutional confusion and tensions in the recent past, which are in part attributed to:

1. Political instability and blight before major elections
2. Reluctance to give a commitment to new structures in the sector, and a legacy of poor inter-agency co-ordination leading to a policy vacuum in the sector
3. No consensus about institutional divisions of responsibilities in the sector and no clearly defined responsibilities for leadership and co-ordination;
4. Uncertainty caused by relocating PNSBC from its current home in INDER, and fear of disrupting the established pace of implementation have limited decision making about PNSBC's future institutional location

Location of PNSBC within INDER has weakened links with the urban sector and led to problems regarding acceptance of institutional responsibilities - informal links with only the water and health sectors has made it difficult to develop long term plans and commitments to establish sustainable co-ordination mechanisms.

Co-ordination

Intersectoral co-ordination is largely informal, and the lack of integrated, formalised and consistent co-ordination places serious constraints on the programme, namely:

- it may lead to duplication of activities and/or contradictory activities
- it places extensive demands on the community in terms of participation

Clearly a need for some restructuring of the sector institutionally is required. Particular significance has been placed on the creation of the Basic Services Section in the Department of Water and Sanitation within the National Directorate for Water. A Co-ordination and Planning Nucleus has been created within DNA/DAS to permit better intersectoral co-ordination and planning for specific low cost sanitation activities with the participation of key agencies (health, physical planning, social action co-ordination, low cost sanitation etc.). Its objectives are to promote and co-ordinate activities for provision of adequate and affordable water and sanitation facilities for low income groups.

Recent developments have placed emphasis on the need to decentralise the operations of the PNSBC. This will involve delegating powers to local municipalities to manage the provincial units, and through greater integration of the private sector in the construction of latrine parts.

Sanitation promotion issues

Guidelines

- Promotion must be matched to the customs, attitudes and knowledge of user communities

- Selection of appropriate communication channels is critical in reaching target audiences and reinforcing core messages. Messages should build on ideas and concepts which are already present in the community. Findings from this research suggest that convenience would be a key issue to target during promotion campaigns for on-plot sanitation

- Community based and managed promotion activities are more effective than externally based interventions

- Interpersonal communication through household visits has proven to be very effective in awareness raising

Background

The development of a sustainable sanitation intervention involves several phases of development, including: surveying, demonstration, consolidation and mobilisation.

This section will focus particularly on the mobilisation phase, on issues relating to effective communication of key messages during the development of a sanitation intervention.

Common aspects of effective sanitation promotion

During the mobilisation phase, promotional activities should be designed and implemented in order to stimulate demand for sanitation facilities, to convince householders that they need to improve their existing facilities, and to demonstrate clearly that they have the skills and means with which to upgrade.

Common elements in effective sanitation promotion initiatives are:

- *Identification of the key target groups to be reached*
  For promotional campaigns to be effectively targeted and adapted, it is necessary to develop an understanding of which groups in a community can benefit most from improved sanitation. Women for instance, have most to do with the operation and maintenance of sanitation, or feel the impact of the lack of sanitation most acutely (i.e., privacy).

- *Identification of the core messages to be communicated*
  This needs to be at the heart of any promotional campaign, and should emphasise the interdisciplinary nature of sanitation, stressing not only technology related issues, but socio-cultural and hygiene concerns. Core messages would typically include a health and hygiene behaviour component, information on the technological options available and why the programme is of importance. The *way* in which core messages are communicated can affect the responsiveness of the community. Excreta disposal is a highly sensitive issue in many cultures, and one in which it is difficult to change behaviour. Communication strategies which are aware of these concerns and adapt to them will reduce the potential for confrontation from the community. Additionally, any communication strategy needs to have a mechanism by which it is possible to judge if core messages have been correctly understood by target groups.

47

- *Awareness of the prevailing socio-cultural framework*
This is critical to understanding why individuals decide to invest in sanitation and how they might respond to a sanitation programmes. The results from this research indicate that the motivation to build facilities on-plot is largely socio-cultural (i.e., status, privacy, or comfort and convenience), rather than from notions of improved health. This does not negate the need for health and hygiene promotion, but demonstrates the importance of designing a promotion campaign which taps into this socio-cultural framework.

- *Consideration of sanitation as a consumer good*
Sanitation facilities require marketing as with any other consumer product. The concept of 'social marketing' offers a comprehensive approach to integrating improvements in water supply and sanitation with the behaviour changes necessary to make these technologies effective in improving public health. In essence, the concept borrows heavily from commercial marketing techniques and applies them to social problems. In relation to sanitation, the social marketing approach implies several key concepts, including: consumer orientation; setting of objectives; the marketing mix (product, place, price and promotion); marketing of environmental influences and exchange theory. A full review of social marketing can be found in Berry, A. (1993).

- *Communication methods*
A mixture of techniques and methods which are adaptable, use existing channels of communication, using simple language and expressions, and which attracts the community's attention are preferable. Findings from Mozambique indicate that those persons charged with communication (animators) were critical factors in the success or otherwise of sanitation promotion campaigns. Common examples of communication methods range from conventional public face-to-face meetings to more innovative campaigns incorporating traditional arts media.

This research has focused on several examples of promotional programmes, and three case studies, with selected comments drawn from semi-structured interviews are reproduced below, illustrating examples of differing approaches and some of the constraints experienced.

Case study 11: Domestic Sanitation Programme, Kumasi, Ghana

Under the Strategic Sanitation Plan for Kumasi, three pilot projects were established, one each covering public latrines in the central business district; simplified sewerage in a high density tenement area and domestic sanitation programme in three residential districts.

Sanitation committees
Committees were established in these districts to promote the programme and to stimulate demand and interest amongst the local population. The role of the committee was four fold: to explain to householders the disadvantages of poor sanitation and the relative benefits of constructing VIP latrines; to administer loan agreements with beneficiaries; to collect monthly loan repayments from householders and to provide feedback to the SSP project team on activities. The committee reserved 2 per cent of the revenue collected to cover their operational costs.

Committees were chosen by consensus and not by election. Membership was determined by several factors, most important of which was a willingness to serve the wider community, and being recognised as a respected community member.

Animation tools
A variety of graphical and audio-visual aids were employed, in addition to demonstration latrines and opening ceremonies for new latrines. Women in particular were used as catalysts for promotion:

"To facilitate hygiene education, a group composed of 20 very influential women in the area was formed in 1991. It is always difficult to get women involved, especially amongst the Muslims; but in showing films and having theatre performances, we had a good chance of attracting them".

Jemima Denis-Antwi, Head of Health Education Division (MoH), Kumasi, Ghana. (UNDP-World Bank Water and Sanitation Programme: RWSG-WA, 1994)

Constraints

In Kumasi, one of the main limitations with the use of sanitation committees was that members were frequently too preoccupied with other community based tasks to maintain the levels of commitment that were required for the committee. Additionally, committee members roles as financial mediators created tension within the community and complicated the tasks of the member in other community based activities.

Case study 12: Programme promotion in Maputo, Mozambique

The National Low Cost Sanitation Programme in Mozambique is a peri-urban programme designed to improve the sanitary conditions of low income urban communities through the promotion of an unreinforced domed slab which covers either a lined or unlined pit.

Animators roles

The programme relies on the activities of sanitary educators, or 'animators' to promote the programme at the community level. Animators are typically drawn from the communities in which they work; are men and women with basic training in health and hygiene behaviour and conduct a variety of outreach activities. Jose Naene, animator for Jorge Dimitrov district in Maputo explains the role of the animator:

"[To] identify the need of the family; the conditions of the family; bring 'propaganda' about the programme; explain how improved latrines work; explain the advantages of improved latrines, the price (that it is cheap); that with these latrines you avoid lots of accidents; that small children can use the latrine; and that the latrines help to avoid disease. The main point is to speak to people and try to convince them [about the improved latrine] and to convince them to dig a pit on their plot for rubbish, how to use water from the well, and to use only necessary fuel.

...when the animators are organising meetings door to door, people ask us to come more often, people agree that the things that we talk about are important and the perception of the latrines is very positive in the community. It does not matter if a family is rich or poor, they all like the latrines. Sometimes perception can depend on the type of soil...there are cases where

a householder should buy a complete latrine but only buys a slab and there are problems. People like the fact that they can upgrade their latrine when they have money ".

Animation activities
In addition to the presence of community based animators, the programme uses a variety of promotional ideas to communicate its messages. These include use of indigenous media (such as employing dance/drama troupes to visit a district) in conjunction with more traditional communication channels (lectures, activists at church and voluntary level, poster campaigns, and radio/television broadcasts). One innovative promotional idea was the distribution of T-shirts, caps and other promotional clothing to publicise the programme. Given the high demand that exists for affordable clothing in Mozambique, this method was an effective way of communicating the programmes' central message (through slogans on the front and rear of the T-shirt).

Constraints
There appeared to be considerable variation in the initiative that individual animators took towards their tasks. It was clear that in some cases, animators had identified key methods by which further promotional activities could be fostered (for example, in some low income districts enterprising householders would ferment and sell locally produced beer, using their plot as a meeting place for the community. The animator in this district had identified this informal 'bar' as a key place in which to promote the improved latrine, allowing people to use and benefit from it at first hand.

Case study 13: Strategic Sanitation Plan, Ouagadougou, Burkina Faso

---

The SSP-O was designed to promote on-site sanitation in Ouagadougou by stimulating demand for upgraded sanitation facilities in two sectors of the city. The project relied on a mixture of animation and social marketing tools.

Workplan
A detailed schedule of activities was devised for the programme, broken into four phases, of which the most relevant in promotional terms were phases 1

and 2:1 - Getting to know the area, 2 - Information campaign. Phase 1 consisted of activities designed to identify key target audiences, leaders and influential persons who would participate in and help advance the programme, whilst Phase 2 focused on presentation of key advocacy messages through public meetings, poster displays and demonstration models.

Animation tools
These relied heavily on a combination of modern communication channels and more indigenous forms of dissemination (ceremonies, district meetings). Radio and television broadcasts were used following survey work to identify *when* most householders listened to broadcast media, *how* many listen, and what *style* of promotional campaign proved most effective. Broadcasts were short in length, avoided a moralistic tone and were timed for peak listening hours.

More unconventional forms of promotion were also adopted. This included dancing troupes performing in dedicated public spaces or the compounds of traditional leaders, competitive football matches organised under the framework of a 'Sanitation Cup' and guided tours to households with latrines built under the programme. This last element proved particularly effective. About 100 tours were organised, allowing those who were interested in the programme, but hesitant, to see at first hand the technology being used. Explanations of the different stages of construction and practical information relating to cost, maintenance and performance could also be given by the host household. Direct interaction in this way had a powerful effect on the attitudes of potential beneficiaries, building trust and confidence in the technology, and acting as a strong stimulus for initiating construction. Following these visits, no visiting householder decided not to build their own household latrine.

Sustaining promotion
The above case studies highlight different approaches to promotion, with slightly different emphasis between each programme. A critical issue is how to maintain enthusiasm for promotion after the initial campaign has run its course. Potential responses to this problem include:

• Developing school sanitation programmes where children learn about environmental sanitation, new technologies, the benefits of improved sanitation, etc. Emmanual Bawa, WES Officer, UNICEF, Accra, Ghana explains his agency's approach to sustaining promotional activities, *"...we tried to focus on schools because our strategy is that you can start this whole awareness campaign with schoolchildren, once they get used to using these facilities at least when they go back to their homes they will be able to say, 'look we have this in school, why can't we have it in the house?'"*.

- The private sector can be used to promote sanitation through the training of local artisans or members of the community to construct local latrines. These artisans can then market their skills in the community and have a financial incentive to widely promote the sanitation programme;
- Develop and introduce new ways of reinforcing core messages. Updating promotional literature, or adapting indigenous media to topical issues will sustain interest in a given message;
- Sanitation promotion campaigns may act as a catalyst for wider community based social development programmes, where local community associations take a more prominent role in environmental activities linked to environmental sanitation;
- Measures such as opening local development offices serve as a focal point between participating groups in the community.

Part 1E:
Conclusions

The following key points emerge from the project's findings concerning on-plot sanitation in low income urban areas.

General

- On-plot sanitation systems are appropriate for low income urban areas. Our findings indicate that a variety of systems are found to be working well on small plot sizes, with limited odour/insect nuisance, without significant operational problems and to the satisfaction of the end user
- There exists a significant gulf between the perceptions of professionals and those of the community when regarding the appropriateness of on-plot sanitation in the urban context. The findings show that professionals' understanding of key issues such as insect/odour nuisance, or the operational problems associated with on-plot systems must be advised by the opinions and perceptions of those who actually use the system.

Specific

- Poverty and indebtedness are key reasons for the absence of household latrine, either constraining the ability of households to save towards the cost of a latrine, or leading to prioritisation of available income to items other than sanitation
- High degrees of user satisfaction were expressed for all latrine types (except bucket/pan latrines); simple pit latrines recorded higher levels of satisfaction than latrines assumed to be of higher technical specification. Satisfaction levels are most significantly affected by smell, insects and emptying problems, although the actual proportion of households recording these points as problems was low
- Small plot size is not a recognisable constraint to the use of household latrines: user satisfaction levels are not significantly affected by plot size, there is little evidence of a link between plot size and technology choice, and few operational problems are directly linked to size of plot

- Odour and insect nuisance is not noted as a significant problem by users, a finding which is reinforced by the low incidence of insects recorded through quantitative testing on different latrine types. The study found that VIP latrines, designed specifically to limit the incidence of insect and odours, actually recorded higher levels of insect/odour related problems amongst users. There is some suggestion that the site of rubbish dumps on the plot may be a more likely source of insect nuisance than the latrine
- The pollution of groundwater from on-plot sanitation is a potential hazard, but not necessarily a risk. Health risks associated with environmental pollution of groundwater must be set against the much greater hazard of widespread open defecation and contamination of the neighbourhood environment with excreta
- Advise householders on the anticipated pit filling/emptying cycle for their latrine type, and that arrangements for emptying are their own responsibility

Details of all these concluding points can be found in the appropriate section of the report.

Part 2

Section 2A
Supporting evidence

Section 2B
Sample characteristics (by technology)

Section 2C
Database listing

Section 2D
Bibliography

Section 2E
Annex

Section 2A
Supporting evidence

Absence of household sanitation

Key findings

- Lack of space is not the primary determinant for absence of household sanitation. Poverty, and/or the inability to save funds to invest in longer term sanitation facilities are key constraints (poverty may force householders to prioritise use of space to other functions)

- Significant family indebtedness, often due to payment of medical fees through illness, constrain ability to save or invest in sanitation

- In cases where plot size was mentioned as the key factor explaining absence, these cases were spread across a range of plot size categories, rather than being exclusively linked to the smallest group

- Plot sizes amongst households without sanitation are not on average smaller than those houses where latrines are present

---

Survey sample

A total of 540 cases (29% of full sample) were found to be lacking any domestic sanitation facilities within the confines of the household plot. The majority of these cases were drawn from Ghana (84%), with India and Mozambique accounting for 14% and 2% of all cases respectively. (*For details, see Sample Characteristics*).

Reasons for absence of household latrines

- In answering the question, '*Why is there no household toilet?*', the largest responses noted 'high cost' (22%); 'use public latrines' (17%); 'lack space' (16%); 'difficult to operate and maintain' (8%); or that 'no facility provided' (6%). [**ref.: absence:1**]

- The response 'lack of space' was not found to be associated exclusively with relatively small plot sizes. Crosstabulations between reason for absence of household latrine and recorded plot size indicate that this factor was evenly represented across all plot size categories, from the

59

smallest grouping 11-220m² (5%), through to the largest grouping 630-2700m² (4%). **[ref.: absence:2]**

- In the majority of cases (86%), the lack of household sanitation facilities was, unsurprisingly, felt to be unsatisfactory. When asked '*What is preferred toilet choice?*', 28% chose WC to septic tank; 18% VIP; 17% simple pit types; 10% WC to sewer; and 8% pour-flush with twin soakpit. A significant minority (5%) expressed that 'any' toilet would be preferred. **[ref.:absence:3]**

Simple pit latrines

Key findings

- Few cases of problems with simple pit latrines recorded, reinforced by high levels of user satisfaction

- User satisfaction levels most significantly affected by smell, emptying and insects

- A quarter of all simple pit latrines had been in use for more than five years

- Only 6% of pit latrines been emptied, most on one occasion only. Re-emptying periods were greater than three years in most cases

---

Description
For a description of simple pit latrines, please refer to section B.

Survey sample
A total of 396 cases (21% of full sample) were found to have a simple pit toilet within the confines of their household plot. The majority of these cases are drawn from Mozambique (86%), with Ghana accounting for the remaining 14%. (*For details, see Sample Characteristics*).

Reasons for construction
- In general, socio-economic factors dictate reasons for construction of simple pits, above purely technical considerations. 'Low cost' (29%) and 'comfort and convenience' (28%) form the two largest responses to the question, '*Why did you build the toilet like this?*'. Other significant minorities included 'easy to clean' (11%), 'simple to use and maintain' (8%) and 'no choice' (6%). **[ref.:simpit:1]**

60

Problems with simple pit latrines
• Notably, just under three-quarters of all cases (73%) indicated that householders had experienced 'no' problems with their simple pit latrine. Where problems were identified, they included 'frequent repairs' (7%); 'smell' (7%); 'smell and insects' (5%); and insects (2%). 'Emptying' ranked as the sixth most important factor with only 1.3%. **[ref.:simpit:2]**

Repairs
• In the majority of cases (85%), users were responsible for repairing their latrine; in 12% of cases, users replied that the latrine had not required repairs to date. **[ref.:simpit:3]**

Cleanliness of latrine
• Surveyors were asked to record the level of cleanliness found in the latrine superstructure (against pre-determined scales). In 86% of cases, latrines were identified as 'very clean' or 'clean', while only 12% were identified as 'not clean' and 2% 'very unclean'. In just under half of the cases sampled, the users claimed to have cleaned the latrine 'today'; just over a third (34%) cleaned 'yesterday' and 17% 'more than 2 days ago'. **[refs.:simpit:4-5]**

Plot size
• Household plot size (m^2) varied in range from a minimum of $28m^2$ to a maximum of $3300m^2$. The arithmetic mean stood at $403m^2$, with a median plot size figure of $306m^2$ and a mode of $375m^2$.

Cost of latrine
• In 98% of all cases, the facility was paid for by the users themselves from their own resources. Monthly operation and maintenance costs ranged from US\$ 0 - US\$ 5 **[ref.:simpit:6-7]**

Years in use
• In the majority of cases sampled (57%), households had been using their latrine for between 1-5 years (of which the majority fall within years 1-3); 18% had been in use for less than 1 year. Notably, a cumulative total of 26% of all cases recorded latrines in use for between 6-31 years (15% between 6-10 years, with the remaining 10% in use between 11-31 years. 80% of this figure was found in years 11-14). **[ref.:simpit:8]**

Pit emptying

- In the majority of cases (94%), simple pits had not been emptied during their lifetime. 2% of the sample showed pits had been emptied once and 1.5% on three occasions. Crosstabulations between years in use against number of times emptied showed that in cases where pits had not been emptied, 59% had been in use for between 1-5 years; 12% for 6-10 years and the remainder (9%) for 11-20 years. **[ref.:simpit:9-10]**

- When asked to judge the volume of sludge removed during emptying, 91% had 'all' pit sludge removed; 4% 'half'; and 2% respectively for both 'quarter' and 'three quarters'. 79% of households maintained that their pit was not yet full. **[ref.:simpit:11]**

- In 58% of all cases the period between pits being emptied lasted for more than 3 years. A re-emptying period of between 5-7 years accounted for the single largest proportion in this grouping (19%). A significant minority of all cases (12%) accounted for re-emptying every six months. **[ref.:simpit:12]**

- Responsibility for emptying simple pit latrines was generally considered to be the householder's (67% of all cases), though significant minorities employed contractors (19%) or perceived the Municipality (14%) to be responsible. **[ref.:simpit:13]**

- The method for emptying simple pit latrines relies to a large extent (61% of cases) on manual action (either by hand or with hand tools). In 30% of cases, a vacuum tanker was used for this purpose. **[ref.:simpit:14]**

- Cost of emptying ranged between US$ 5 to US$ 40 per emptying incident. **[ref.:simpit:15]**

- After emptying, the majority of households reported that pit contents were buried on-plot (60%); 24% stated that hygienic disposal off-site occurred, and 11% that indiscriminate dumping away from the plot was the main practice. **[ref.:simpit:16]**

- Of those households which identified emptying as a problem, 28% noted 'high cost', and 17% 'frequency' of emptying. 50% claimed 'no' problems with the process. **[ref.:simpit:17]**

Anal cleansing
- In the majority of cases, 'newspaper' was used as anal cleansing material (65%); toilet paper by 20% and 7% a combination of both. [ref.:simpit:18] Following defecation, the majority of users placed their cleansing materials either into a receptacle inside the latrine shelter (58%); outside the shelter (21%) or in the pit itself (21%). [ref.:simpit:19] In those cases where the material did not end up in the pit or receptacle inside/outside the shelter, it was burnt. [ref.:simpit:20]

Odour and insect nuisance
- Simple pit latrines recorded little or moderate odour and insect nuisance levels. When users were asked to express on a pre-determined scale the extent to which the pit smelt, 54% of households recorded 'no smell'; 37% 'slight smell'; and 9% 'strong smell' [ref.:simpit:21] A similar question relating to insect nuisance (flies) found that 91% of householders considered there to be either 'no' or 'tens' of flies; 8% 'hundreds' and 1% 'thousands'. [ref.:simpit:22]

User satisfaction
- High degrees of user satisfaction were expressed with simple pit latrines. 90% of all householders responded that they were either 'satisfied' or 'very satisfied' with their pit latrine. Of the remainder, 6% recorded being 'unsatisfied', and only 1% 'very unsatisfied'. [ref.:simpit:23]

- User satisfaction levels were not significantly affected by the incidence of either smell or odour nuisance in percentage terms. [ref.:simpit:25-26] However, of all the problems identified with simple pit latrines, 'smell', 'emptying' and a combination of smell and insects were found to have the greatest impact on these satisfaction levels. [ref.:simpit:27]

Identified problems and their perceived impact
- Critically, of those users who identified that there were problems with their simple pit, very few considered this to have more than a 'moderate impact' on their ability to use the facility (5%). The majority (84%) felt that the problem(s) identified had 'no impact'. [ref.:simpit:24] It was found that the factors which would most help to relieve the identified problems recorded included 'lower cost' (41%); 'easier to operate and maintain' (35%) and 'not require regular emptying' (10%) [ref.:simpit:28]

63

Ventilated Improved Pit (VIP) latrines

Key findings

- Insect and odour nuisance recorded as common problems with the VIP latrine
- A third of all VIP latrines had been in use for more than five years
- A significant proportion of VIP latrines required emptying every six months
- High levels of user satisfaction expressed, but satisfaction levels affected most by incidence of smell, insects and emptying problems

Description

For a description of ventilated improved pit latrines, please refer to section B.

Survey sample

A total of 52 cases (3% of full sample) were found to have a VIP toilet within the confines of their household plot. All of these cases were drawn from Ghana. (*For details, see Sample Characteristics*).

Reasons for construction

- Social reasons act as the primary reason for construction of VIP latrines, with 'comfort and convenience' (34%) ranking as the largest response to the question, '*Why did you build the toilet like this?*'. Other significant minorities included 'low cost' (12%), 'no choice' (12%), 'simple to use and maintain' (8%), 'lack water' (8%) and a combination of 'comfort and convenience' and 'health and hygiene' (8%) [ref.:vip:1]

Problems with VIP latrines

- 52% of all cases indicated that householders have experienced 'no' problems with their VIP latrines. Ironically for a latrine designed to reduce insect and odour nuisance these factors figured prominently amongst responses. A combination of 'smell and insects' (10%); 'emptying' (8%); 'insects' (6%); and 'smell' (4%) ranking as the most common problems noted [ref.:vip:2]

Repairs

- In the majority of cases (94%), the householder was responsible for repairing the latrine. [ref.:vip:3]

64

Cleanliness of latrine

* Surveyors were asked to record the level of cleanliness found in the latrine superstructure (against pre-determined scales); 23% of cases were identified as 'very clean'; 65% as 'clean'; and 13% as 'not clean'. In just over three-quarters (77%) of the cases sampled, the users claimed to have cleaned the latrine 'today'; 10% cleaned 'yesterday' and 13% 'more than 2 days ago'. [refs.:vip:4-5]

Plot size

* Household plot size (m^2) varied in range from a minimum of 60m^2 to a maximum of 4500m^2. The arithmetic mean stood at 825m^2, with a median plot size figure of 630m^2 and a mode of 630m^2.

Cost

* In 52% of all cases, the facility was paid for by the users themselves from their own resources, with loans accounting for an additional 13%. A third of households spent nothing on monthly maintenance; 25% spending 5000 cedis (US$2.4); 12% 4000 cedis (US$1.9). [ref.:vip:6]

Years in use

* In the majority of cases sampled (59%), households had been using their VIP latrine for between 1-5 years; 9% for less than 1 year; and 33% for between 6-10 years. [ref.:vip:7]

Pit emptying

* In 46% of cases, VIP latrines had not been emptied during their lifetime. 22% of the sample showed latrines had been emptied once and 16% twice. Crosstabulations between years in use against number of times emptied showed that in cases where VIP latrines had not been emptied, 31% had been in use for between 1-5 years; and 6% for 6-10 years. [ref.:vip:8-9]

* When asked to judge the volume of sludge removed during emptying, 57% of householders had 'all' pit sludge removed; 6% respectively for both 'half' and 'three quarters' and 3% for 'quarter'. 29% of households claimed that the pits were not yet full. [ref.:vip:10]

* In 17% of all cases the period between pits being emptied lasted for more than 3 years. Re-emptying periods of 1 and 2 years accounted for 21% respectively. Significantly, 42% of all cases accounted for re-emptying every 6 months. [ref.:vip:11]

- Responsibility for emptying VIP latrines was generally perceived to be that of the municipality (54%), though significant minorities employed contractors for emptying (26%) or undertook emptying themselves (20%). **[ref.:vip:12]**

- The method for emptying VIP latrines relies on heavily on vacuum tankers (53%) or manually with hand tools (38%). **[ref.:vip:13]**

- In cases where householders possessed knowledge about the cost of emptying (n=16), values ranged widely from between 4000 to 50,000 cedis (US$2-24). The most common cost figure noted for emptying was 30,000 cedis, or US$15 **[ref:vip:14]**

- Following emptying, 89% of households report that pit contents were disposed hygienically off-site; 7% dumped indiscriminately away from the plot; and 4% buried on-plot; **[ref.:vip:15]**

- Of those households which identified emptying as a problem, 45% noted 'high cost', and 5% respectively for combinations of 'high cost and frequency' and 'high cost and hygiene'. 45% claimed 'no' problems with the process. **[ref.:vip:16]**

Anal cleansing
- 'Newspaper' was used as anal cleansing material in 51% of cases; toilet paper by 16% and 31% a combination of both. **[ref.:vip:17]** Following defecation, the majority of users placed their cleansing materials either into a receptacle inside the latrine shelter (96%); or outside the shelter (4%). **[ref.:vip:18]** In those cases where the material did not end up in the pit or receptacle inside/outside the shelter, it was burnt. **[ref.:vip:19]**

Odour and insect nuisance
- VIP latrines recorded relatively high degrees of odour nuisance levels. When asked to express on a pre-determined scale to what extent the VIP latrine smelt, 40% of households recorded 'no smell'; 54% 'slight smell'; and 6% 'strong smell' **[ref.:vip:20]** A similar question relating to insect nuisance (flies) showed that for 90% of householders there was either 'no' or 'tens' of flies. However, for categories acting as indicators of higher levels of nuisance, VIP latrines performed poorly, with 3% and 7% of all cases recording 'hundreds' and 'thousands' of flies respectively. **[ref.:vip:21]**

Photograph 1:
Typical latrine superstructure (made from reeds) used in Mozambique, where it is customary for latrine shelters to be built without a roof

Photograph 2:
Transportation of completed slabs from production unit to household plot, Maputo, Mozambique

67

Photograph 3:
Production of popular unreinforced domed slabs used for low cost simple pit latrines in peri-urban areas of Mozambique

Photograph 4:
Pour flush latrine in improved urban slum, Vijayawada, India. Operational sanitation
facilities were found to be commonplace on the smallest of plot sizes (as small as 14m²)

User satisfaction
- Relatively high degrees of user satisfaction were expressed. 83% of all householders responded that they were either 'satisfied' or 'very satisfied' with their VIP latrine. Of the remainder, 8% recorded being 'unsatisfied', and only 2% 'very unsatisfied'. **[ref.:vip:22]**

- User satisfaction does not seem to be significantly affected by the incidence of either smell or odour in percentage terms **[ref.:vip:23-24]**, but 'smell', 'insects' and a combination of smell, insects and emptying do make the most prominent impact of all identified problems to satisfaction levels **[ref.:vip:25]**

Identified problems and their perceived impact
- Notably, of those users who identified that there were problems with their VIP latrines, few considered this to have more than a 'moderate impact' on their ability to use the facility (18%). The majority (61%) felt that the problem(s) identified had 'no impact', with 21% recording 'slight impact'. **[ref.:vip:26]** It was found that the factors which would most help to relieve the identified problems recorded included 'lower cost' (36%); 'easier to operate and maintain' (41%) and 'not require regular emptying' (9%) **[ref.:vip:27]**

Pour-flush latrines

Key findings

- Pour flush latrines have been constructed on plots as small as 14m²

- Just under two-thirds of all households using pour-flush latrines had used them for more than five years

- Two-thirds of all latrines had not been emptied, and half of these had been in use for between 6-10 years

- For 60% of all latrines the period between being emptied exceeded three years. In just over a quarter latrines, this period lasted for five years or more

- User satisfaction levels are most significantly affected by smell, blockage and frequent repairs

---

Description
For a description of pour-flush pit latrines, please refer to section B.

Survey sample

A total of 394 cases (21% of full sample) were found to have a pour flush toilet within the confines of their household plot. All of these cases are drawn from India. (*For details, see Sample Characteristics*).

Reasons for construction

- Socio-economic factors tend to determine the reasons for construction of pour-flush latrines. 'Comfort and convenience' (34%), 'Low cost' (21%); 'no choice' (15%) and 'easy to clean' (11%) form the largest responses to the question, '*Why did you build the toilet like this?*'. **[ref.:pf:1]**

Problems with pour-flush latrines

- 59% of all cases indicated that householders had experienced 'no' problems with their pour-flush latrines. Where problems were identified, they included 'smell' (12%); 'insects' (8%); 'blockage' (5%) and 'emptying' (4%) **[ref.:pf:2]**

Repairs

- In the majority of cases (95%), users were responsible for repairing their latrine, the remainder being split between the Municipality (3%) and 'other agency' (1%). **[ref.:pf:3]**

Cleanliness of latrine

- Surveyors were asked to record the level of cleanliness found in the latrine superstructure (against pre-determined scales). 87% of cases were identified as 'very clean' or 'clean'; with 8% as 'not clean' and 4% 'very unclean'. In 39% of the cases sampled, the users claimed to have cleaned the latrine 'today'; 11% cleaned 'yesterday' and 50% 'more than 2 days ago'. **[refs.:pf:4-5]**

Plot size

- Household plot size (m²) varied in range from a minimum of 14m² to a maximum of 3374m². The arithmetic mean stood at 146m², the median plot size figure of 90m² and a mode of 54m².

Cost

- In 43% of all cases, the facility was paid for by the users themselves from their own resources, with 'loan and subsidy' accounting for 47%. **[ref.:pf6]**
  Of those who knew how many months of their loan were left to repay

(n=75), 17% of households had 20 months to repay; 9% had eight months left to pay; and 33% had between 2-6 months left to complete. **[ref.:pf:7]** Monthly maintenance costs were low (ranging between Rs10-Rs100 (US$0.30-US$2.8), with most households spending either Rs10-20 per month (25% and 27% of all cases respectively). 9% of households spent nothing on maintenance. **[ref.:pf:8]**

Years in use
• In 36% of cases, households had been using their pour-flush latrines for between 1-5 years; 47% for between 6-10 years; 12% between 11-20 years and 3% for longer. Only 3% of cases had used their latrine for less than 1 year. **[ref.:pf:9]**

Pit emptying
• In 66% of cases, pour flush latrines had not been emptied during their lifetime. 20% of the sample showed latrines had been emptied once and 8% twice. Crosstabulations between years in use against number of times emptied show that in cases where pour-flush latrines had not been emptied, 41% had been in use for between 1-5 years; and 47% for 6-10 years. Where latrines had been emptied once, 64% had been in use for 6-10 years **[ref.:pf:10-11]**

• When asked to judge the volume of sludge removed during emptying, 64% of householders responded that pits were not yet full. Where emptying had occurred (n=101) 78% of households had 'all' pit sludge removed; 15% 'half'; 6% 'quarter' and 1% 'three-quarters'. **[ref.:pf:12-13]**

• In 59% of all cases the period between pits being emptied lasted for 3 years or more (with 27% of cases falling in the 'more than 5 years' category). A two year re-emptying period accounted for 21% of cases and one year, 10%. **[ref.:pf:14]**

• Responsibility for emptying pour flush latrines was generally perceived to be that of the user (81%). **[ref.:pf:15]**

• The method for emptying pour flush latrines relies exclusively on manual techniques, either by hand (41%) or with hand tools (59%) **[ref.:pf:16]**

- In cases where householders possessed knowledge about the cost of emptying (n=98), values ranged from between Rs150-1500 (US$4.0-42.0). The most common figure noted was Rs500 (US$14). [ref:pf:17]

- Following emptying, 75% of households reported that pit contents were dumped off-site; in 15% of cases pit excreta was disposed hygienically off-site and in 8% of cases it was composted [ref.:pf:18]

- Of those households which identified emptying as a problem, 29% noted 'high cost', and 14 'hygiene'. 46% claimed 'no' problems with the process. 'Frequency' and 'access to plot' accounted for only 5% and 4% respectively. [ref.:pf:19]

Odour and insect nuisance
- Pour-flush latrines recorded little odour and insect nuisance. Users were asked to express on a pre-determined scale to what extent the pour flush latrine smelt. 63% of cases recorded 'no smell'; 30% 'slight smell'; and 6% 'strong smell' [ref.:pf:20] A similar question relating to insect nuisance (flies) found that 95% of householders considered there to be either 'no' or 'tens' of flies; with the remaining 5% noting 'hundreds'. [ref.:pf:21]

User satisfaction
- High degrees of user satisfaction were expressed with pour-flush latrines. 83% of all householders responded that they were either 'satisfied' or 'very satisfied' with their latrine. [ref.:pf:22]

- User satisfaction does not seem to be significantly affected by the incidence of either smell or odour in percentage terms [ref.:pf:23-24], but 'smell', 'blockage' and 'frequent repairs' make the most prominent impact of all identified problems to satisfaction levels [ref.:pf:25]

Identified problems and their perceived impact
- Where users identified that there were problems with their latrines, few considered this to have more than a 'moderate impact' on their ability to use the facility (11%). The majority (69%) felt that the problem(s) identified had 'no impact', with 20% recording 'slight impact'. [ref.:pf:26] It was found that the factors which would most help to relieve the identified problems recorded included 'easier to operate and maintain' (43%); 'lower cost' (27%); and 'not require regular emptying' (17%) [ref.:pf:27]

WC to septic tank

Key findings

- The most common problems noted with septic tanks include 'lack of water' and 'emptying'. These two issues most significantly impact on user satisfaction levels

- 58% of all households had used septic tanks for more than three years. 36% of these had used the facility for more than 11 years

- Just under half of all septic tanks had not been emptied during their lifetime

- In just over one third of all cases, the period between emptying the tanks exceeded three years. Interestingly, a significant proportion complained of the need to empty every six months

- High degrees of user satisfaction expressed

Description

For a description of septic tanks, please refer to section B.

Survey sample

A total of 159 cases (9% of full sample) were found to have a WC to septic tank within their household plot. 82% of these cases are drawn from Ghana, the remainder from India. (*For details, see Sample Characteristics*).

Reasons for construction

- Social factors tend to determine reasons for construction of septic tanks. 'Comfort and convenience' (48%), and a combination of 'comfort and convenience' and 'health and hygiene' (6%) form the largest positive responses to the question, '*Why did you build the toilet like this?*'. 22% of households indicate that they had 'no choice' in building septic tanks, which may refer to users buying plots on which this type of facility was already provided. The relative expense of septic tanks is indicated by the low response to 'low cost' (2%) **[ref.:wcsep:1]**

Problems with septic tanks

- 54% of all cases indicated that householders had experienced 'no' problems with their septic tanks. Where problems were identified, they included 'lack water' (12%); 'emptying' (12%); 'insects' (5%) and 'blockage' (5%) **[ref.:wcsep:2]**

Repairs

- In most cases (82%), the householder was responsible for repairing their toilet. Other significant minorities including 'contractor' (8%), and in 8% of all cases responded the septic tank had 'not needed repair' [ref.:wcsep:3]

Cleanliness of latrine

- Surveyors were asked to record the level of cleanliness found in the latrine superstructure (against pre-determined scales). In 19% of cases, latrines were identified as 'very clean'; with 72% as 'clean'. In 44% of the cases sampled, the users claimed to have cleaned the latrine 'today'; 8% cleaned 'yesterday' and 48% 'more than 2 days ago'. [refs.:wcsep:4-5]

Plot size

- Household plot size (m^2) varied in range from a minimum of $27m^2$ to a maximum of $4500m^2$. The arithmetic mean stood at $650m^2$, the median plot size figure of $576m^2$ and a mode of $900m^2$.

Cost

- In 71% of all cases, the facility was paid for by the users themselves from their own resources. [ref.:wcsep:6] Monthly maintenance costs ranged from US$ 0.30 to US$ 10 [ref.:wcsep:7]

Years in use

- In 36% of cases, households had been using their septic tanks for between 1-5 years; 22% for between 6-10 years; 18% between 11-20 years and 18% for longer. 6% of cases had used their latrine for less than 1 year [ref.:wcsep:8]

Emptying

- In 48% of cases, septic tanks had not been emptied during their lifetime. 12% of the sample showed tanks had been emptied once and 8% twice. Crosstabulations between years in use and number of times emptied show that in cases where septic tanks had not been emptied, 80% had been in use for between 0-5 years; and 12% for 6-10 years. Where tanks had been emptied once, 36% had been in use for 0-5 years and 27% for 6-10 years [ref.:wcsep:9-10]

- When asked to judge the volume of sludge removed during emptying, 35% of householders responded that the tank was not yet full. Where emptying had occurred (n=80) 85% of households had 'all' tank sludge removed; 7% 'half'; and 6% 'three-quarters'. [ref.:wcsep:11-12]

- In 34% of all cases the period between tanks being emptied lasted for 3 years or more (with 21% of cases being accounted by the 3-5 years category). Other significant responses include 'every 6 months' (23%); 'every 2 years' (18%) and 'every year' (13%). **[ref.:wcsep:13]**

- In response to the question *Who is responsible for emptying the pit/tank/ toilet?*, 51% accounted responsibility to the Municipality; 29% to the user and 19% to contractors. **[ref.:wcsep:14]**

- The method for emptying septic tanks relies predominantly the use of vacuum tankers (80%). Manual emptying accounts for the remaining 20%, by hand recording 11% and with machinery 8%**[ref.:wcsep:15]**

- Cost of emptying ranged from US$ 8 to US$18 **[ref:wcsep:16]**

- Following emptying, just under half (49%) of all households report that tank contents are dumped off-site; 45% claim hygienic disposal off-site and 4% buried on plot **[ref.:wcsep:17]**

- Of those households which identified emptying as a problem, 12% noted 'high cost', and 10% 'access to plot'. 60% claimed 'no' problems with the process. **[ref.:wcsep:18]**

Odour and insect nuisance
- Users were asked to express on a pre-determined scale to what extent the septic tanks smelt. 67% of cases recorded 'no smell'; 32% 'slight smell'; and 1% 'strong smell' **[ref.:wcsep:19]** A similar question relating to insect nuisance (flies) found that 79% of householders considered there to be 'no', and the remaining 21% 'tens' of flies. **[ref.:wcsep:20]**

User satisfaction
- High degrees of user satisfaction were expressed. 90% of all householders responded that they were either 'satisfied' or 'very satisfied' with their septic tank. **[ref.:wcsep:21]**

- User satisfaction does not seem to be significantly affected by the incidence of either insects or odour in percentage terms **[ref.:wcsep:22-23]**, but 'lack of water', and 'emptying' make the most prominent impact of all identified problems to satisfaction levels **[ref.:wcsep:24]**

Identified problems and their perceived impact
- Where users identified that there were problems with their latrines, few considered this to have more than a 'moderate impact' on their ability to

76

use the facility (14%). The majority (86%) felt that the problem(s) identified had either 'no impact' or 'slight impact', [ref.:wcsep:25]

- It was found that the factors which would most help to relieve the identified problems recorded included 'easier to operate and maintain' (46%); 'regular water supply' (13%), 'not require regular emptying' (11%), and 'lower cost' (10%); [ref.:wcsep:26]

Bucket/pan latrines

Key findings

- Emptying is the most commonly noted problem with bucket/pan latrines, especially the frequency and cost elements. Smell and insect nuisance are of secondary importance

- A quarter of all bucket/pan latrines have been in use for between 21-30 years

- Bucket/pan latrines record the highest levels of insect and odour nuisance of all latrine types

- Users expressed a high degree of dissatisfaction with bucket/pan latrines. Satisfaction is significantly affected by smell, insects and emptying practices

Description
For a description of bucket/pan latrines, please refer to section B.

Survey sample
A total of 264 cases (14% of full sample) were found to have a bucket/pan latrine within the confines of their household plot. All of these cases are drawn from Ghana. (*For details, see Sample Characteristics*).

Reasons for construction
- In general, factors beyond user control and cost considerations determine the main reasons for construction of bucket/pan latrines. 'No choice' accounts for 39% of cases, reflecting the fact that many bucket/pan latrines were built with the house, and 'low cost' accounts for 28% of responses. Other significant minorities included 'comfort and convenience' (12%), and 'simple to use and maintain' (8%). [ref.:bucket:1]

Problems with bucket/pan latrines
- 'Emptying' represents the single most common problem with bucket/pan latrines (accounting for 42% of all responses), followed by a combination of smell and emptying (9%); smell, insects and emptying (6%) and emptying and expense (5%). 'Smell' and 'insects', problems which are typically associated with bucket/pan latrines, accounted for only 4% and 0.4% respectively **[ref.:bucket:2]**

Repairs
- For the majority of cases (96%), users were responsible for repairing their latrine; in 2% of cases, users replied that the latrine had not required repairs to date. **[ref.:bucket:3]**

Cleanliness of latrine
- Surveyors were asked to record the level of cleanliness found in the latrine superstructure (against pre-determined scales). In roughly half of all cases, bucket/pan latrines were identified as 'clean', with a slightly smaller figure (43%) recorded as 'not clean'. In 39% of the cases sampled, users claimed to have cleaned the latrine 'today'; 21% cleaned 'yesterday' and 40% 'more than 2 days ago'. **[refs.:bucket:4-5]**

Plot size
- Household plot size (m^2) varied in range from a minimum of 70m^2 to a maximum of 5772m^2. The arithmetic mean stood at 695m^2, the median plot size figure of 600m^2 and a mode of 630m^2.

Cost of latrine
- In 74% of all cases, the facility was paid by the users from their own resources, and in 4% the cost was met through a subsidy. The 20% 'not known' figure reflects the number of bucket/pan latrines originally built with the house **[ref.:bucket:6]** Monthly operation and maintenance costs ranged from 0 to 40,000 cedis (US$ 0-US$ 20), with a mean figure of 5346 cedis (US$ 3). **[ref.:bucket:7]**

Years in use
- With the history of bucket/pan latrine use in Ghana, the figures for years in use reflect an older age range than other latrine types. In 25% of cases, households had been using their latrine for between 21-30 years; 22% of

cases for between 11-20 years; and 23% of cases for between 1-10 years. [ref.:bucket:8]

Emptying

- For bucket/pan latrines, the most common interval for emptying is between two and three days (19% and 42% respectively). Other significant minorities include 'weekly' (14%) and 'every 4 days' (8%). [ref.:bucket:9]

- Responsibility for emptying bucket/pans was seen to be the responsibility of 'contractors' (63%), though 29% saw this as the users duty and 8% perceived the Municipality to be responsible. [ref.:bucket:10]

- In 99% of all cases, users were responsible for paying for emptying services. [ref:bucket:11]

- After emptying, 41% of households claimed that bucket/pan contents were dumped indiscriminately off-site; 25% claimed hygienic disposal off-site, and 3% buried on-plot. 31% householders responded 'not known'. [ref.:bucket:12]

- Of those households which identified emptying as a problem, 'frequency' of emptying was the single most important factor (46%); 9% of households recorded 'high cost' as a problem. 38% claimed 'no' problems with emptying. [ref.:bucket:13]

Anal cleansing

- In 49% of cases, 'newspaper' was used as anal cleansing material; 29% a combination of both newspaper and toilet paper; and 'toilet paper' alone accounted for 8%. [ref.:bucket:14] Following defecation, the majority of users placed their cleansing material either into a receptacle inside the latrine shelter (91%); or in the bucket/pan itself (5%), or outside the shelter (1%). [ref.:bucket:15] In those cases where the material did not end up in the bucket/pan or receptacle inside/outside the shelter, it was burnt (92%) or put on a rubbish dump (8%). [ref.:bucket:16]

Odour and insect nuisance

- Bucket/pan latrines were found to suffer from significant insect and odour nuisance, as measured by the users themselves. Householders were asked

79

to express on a pre-determined scale to what extent the bucket/pan smelt. Only 10% of cases recorded 'no smell'; the majority (70%) noting 'slight smell'; and 20% 'strong smell' [ref.:bucket:17] A similar question relating to insect nuisance (flies) found that 20% of householders considered there to be 'no' flies; 68% 'tens' of flies; 10% 'hundreds' and 3% 'thousands'. [ref.:bucket:18] In cases where households responded to questions about presence of cockroaches (n=122), 60% indicated 'tens' of cockroaches in the latrine shelter, the remainder reporting 'none'. [ref:bucket:19]

User satisfaction

- Relatively high degrees of user dissatisfaction were expressed about bucket/pan latrines. 48% of all householders responded that they were either 'very unsatisfied' or 'unsatisfied' with their bucket/pan latrine. Of the remainder, 29% recorded being 'satisfied', and only 4% 'very satisfied'. [ref.:bucket:20]

- Although smell and odour were recorded as problems of secondary importance to emptying, user satisfaction levels were significantly affected by them. Crosstabulations for satisfaction against smell indicate that 47% of all cases correspond with the variables 'very unsatisfied / unsatisfied' and 'slight/strong smell'. Similarly, 44% of all cases correspond with the variables 'very unsatisfied / unsatisfied' and 'tens, hundreds and thousands' of flies. [ref.:bucket:21-22]

- 'Emptying' (21%), 'smell' (2.3%) and a combination of 'smell and emptying' (7%) and 'smell, insects and emptying' (4%) have the most prominent impacts of all identified problems to user satisfaction levels [ref.:bucket:23]

Identified problems and their perceived impact

- Of those users who identified that there were problems with their bucket/pan, only 16% considered that the problem(s) had no impact. A large proportion (49%) felt that the problem(s) identified were of 'moderate impact' or higher. [ref.:bucket:24] It was found that the factors which would most help to relieve these problems included 'not require regular emptying' (32%); 'simpler toilet design' (26%); 'easier to operate and maintain' (17%); and 'lower cost' (9%). [ref.:bucket:25]

Plot size

Key findings

- Operational sanitation facilities were found to be commonplace on the smallest of plot sizes

- Levels of user satisfaction were not significantly affected by the incidence of small plot size

- There is little indication that plot size determines technology choice. No definitive grouping or concentration of technology types was observed by recorded size categories

- There is little indication that plot size is associated with particular operational problems. Where the most common latrine problems were noted, they were spread across all size categories

- The absence of household sanitation is not exclusive to the smallest plot sizes

---

Background
Critics of pit latrines often claim they are unsuitable for small plots in urban areas. In Jamaica, regulations prohibited pit latrine construction in areas where the density was higher than ten houses per acre (23 houses per hectare); in Indonesia, regulations state that areas with over 250 persons per hectare shall be classified as densely populated and shall not use on-plot excreta disposal (Alaerts and others, 1991). In a manual prepared for Habitat it was stated that the pit latrine system (except VIP's) is 'unsuitable for use in even low density urban developments' (Roberts, 1987). The smallest plot size recommended for twin pit pour flush latrines in India is 26 square metres (Riberio, 1985). None of the criteria used appear to be based on reasoned argument or on evidence of performance.

Household survey results and lessons

On-plot sanitation unsuitable for small plot sizes?
Significant proportions of sample households **with** operational sanitation facilities were found on relatively small plot sizes: one third of all such cases were measured with plot areas of up to 150m²; just over 10 per cent on plots with an area not greater than 54m² [ref:all:1]. Although this indicates the coincidence of domestic sanitation on relatively small plots, it fails to say anything about the performance or suitability of the facilities. Although not a perfect measure of 'suitability', levels of user satisfaction are indicative. When asked to express degrees of (dis)satisfaction with their facility, those

81

households with the smallest plot sizes (defined here as in the range 13-110m²) expressed high levels of satisfaction, 83% being either 'satisfied' or 'very satisfied' with their facility, with13% either 'unsatisfied' or 'very unsatisfied'. [ref:all:2] Importantly, in crosstabulations between satisfaction levels and recorded problems with latrines, lack of space does not feature amongst the most commonly noted problems [ref:all:3].

Plot size determines technology choice?

Table 2 below shows the incidence of selected technology types against their respective plot size categories. Critically, it indicates that technology choice is not exclusively matched to a single plot size category. Although some technology types have higher concentrations within a specific plot size range (i.e., pour flush latrines and the 13-100m² range), significant minorities also fall within other size categories.

Table 2: Incidence of technology type against plot size category				
	Plot size category			
Count Row %	13-110m²	111-300m²	301-598m²	599m²·highest
Bucket/pan	2 0.8	22 8.5	101 39.0	134 51.7
Simple pit		15 21.4	18 25.7	37 52.9
VIP	1 4.0	1 4.0	6 24.0	17 68.0
Double pit			5 20.0	20 80.0
WC - sewer	15 50.0	7 23.3	3 10.0	5 16.7
WC - septic tank	22 14.2	12 7.7	44 28.4	77 49.7
Pour flush x 2	185 71.7	59 22.9	7 2.7	7 2.7
Pour flush x 1	84 70.0	30 25.0		6 5.0
Improved latrine	7 2.2	167 54.2	122 39.6	12 3.8

Key: *Count*: number of cases in each category
Row %: cell percentage as an expression of row total

Operational problems associated with small plot sizes?
The findings indicate that problems associated with low cost sanitation in urban areas are common across different plot size categories. Where problems were noted, the incidence of the three most important, 'emptying', 'smell' and 'insects', were found to be dispersed across all four size categories **[ref.: all:3]**

Absence of household latrines a function of small plot size?
Households **without** sanitation facilities are not exclusively concentrated on the smallest plot sizes. A median plot size figure of 432m² (table 3 below) indicates that 50 per cent of these cases are found above this mid-point in plot size categories (up to a maximum of 2700m²). Furthermore, the distribution of plot sizes for households without sanitation tends to be skewed towards larger plot categories, as the mode figure of 630m² indicates. Mean, median and modal plot sizes for households without sanitation are larger than in cases where either a simple pit or pour-flush latrine is in use.

Postal survey results and lessons

The responses obtained from sector professionals through the postal survey in large part confirm the findings from the household survey. The postal survey was based on a sample of 57.

Role of planning regulations and minimum plot size
Respondents to the postal survey were asked to estimate the minimum plot sizes in their city as specified in planning regulations. As to be expected, this

Table 3: Plot size calculations for selected technology types					
	Plot sizes (m²)				
Type	Mean	Median	Mode	Minimum	Maximum
Pour flush	146	90	54	14	3374
Simple pit	403	306	375	28	3300
None	466	432	630	11	2700
WC septic tank	650	576	900	27	4500
Bucket	695	600	630	70	5772
VIP	825	630	630	60	4500

Table 4: Comparison between minimum plot sizes laid down in planning regulation and average plot sizes in informally developed urban districts

| | Plot sizes (m^2) | | | | |
	Mean	Median	Mode	Minimum	Maximum
Minimum plot size*	500	387	150	36	2500
Average plot size	419	220	150	35	3600

*As laid down in planning regulations

figure was found to be consistently larger than average plot sizes in informally planned urban districts, as table 4 above indicates.

Variations in systems used according to formal/informal development
Comparisons between technology types most commonly used in planned and unplanned urban areas confirms what is previously known. In more formally planned and better serviced districts there is a tendency towards use of WC toilets (either to sewers or septic tanks), whilst in more informally and haphazardly planned districts, non-flush systems such as simple pit latrines, VIP's, or no facility are common. For both formally and informally planned districts however, a diversity of technology types in use was noted. **[ref.:post:1-2]**

Odour and insect nuisance

Key findings

- Only small percentages of households perceive odour and insect nuisance to be a common problem with their latrine (although nuisance of this kind does have a significant impact on satisfaction levels)

- Bucket/pan latrines register the highest nuisance levels of all latrine types

- Relative to other latrine types VIP's record higher than anticipated levels of odour and insect nuisance. There is little conclusive evidence to suggest a link between odour and insect nuisance and: height of vent above roof line, presence of fly screens, vent pipe colour and diameter of pipe

- Quantitative test results for insect nuisance indicate low absolute numbers of insects observed across a range of latrine types

- Anecdotal evidence raises doubts about domestic latrines as the primary source of insect nuisance on-plot

Background
Complaints about pit latrines most frequently mention odours and insect nuisance, yet there are few specific references to overcoming these nuisances in urban areas. Flies are a serious problem because they spread disease through feeding and breeding on faeces. Some types of mosquitoes (the *Culex* variety) breed in polluted water such as in wet latrines and may carry the disease filariasis. Reduction of smells, flies and mosquitoes are therefore of the greatest importance to reducing household and environmental health hazards.

General incidence of insects and odour nuisance
Odour and insect nuisance are the second and third most commonly noted problems mentioned by users of latrines in urban areas. However, percentages in both cases are small (accounting for only 7% and 4% of cases for 'smell' and 'insects' respectively), with 'emptying' being the single most frequently noted problem (12%) **[ref:all:4]**

Incidence of odour nuisance by latrine type
Table 5 below compares householder responses by latrine type for the question *'Does the toilet smell? How bad is this smell?'* It is important to note how few of the responses fall under the 'strong smell' category. What is unusual are the responses for both simple pits and VIP latrines; with the former registering larger percentages under 'no smell' and smaller percentages under the 'slight smell' categories than the VIP latrine type. Previous assumptions about simple pit vis-à-vis VIP latrines would tend to question

Table 5: User perception of the incidence of odour nuisance, by latrine type

		Odour nuisance (% of cases)		
Latrine type	Cases	No smell	Slight smell	Strong smell
Bucket/pan	253	10	70	20
Simple pits	388	54	37	9
VIP	48	40	54	6
Pour flush	391	63	30	6
WC to septic tank	152	67	32	1
All latrine types		49	42	9

such a finding especially given that VIP latrines had been designed specifically to address the problem of odour nuisance. One possible explanation may be that the odour problems in VIP latrines are exacerbated by increased fouling around the squat hole due to the dark interior of the latrine.

Use of vent pipes

The study looked at VIP latrines with vent pipes in order to assess their effectiveness in controlling insect and odour nuisance. In general, the statements already made concerning user perception of odours and insects to some extent answer this question. Incorrect siting of the vent pipe below the roof level is assumed to reduce the efficacy of the vent. However, this research found no significant relationship between vent pipe height above (or below) existing roof level and perceived odour nuisance. **[ref:vip:28]** Similarly, crosstabulations between the incidence of insects in the latrine and the presence and condition of a fly screen failed to show trends which might indicate some relationship between the two variables. **[ref:vip:29]** Further analysis on odour nuisance based on vent pipe colour and diameter of vent pipe proved equally inconclusive. **[ref:vip:30-31]**

However, the sample size involved with VIP latrines was small (n=52) and the results must be interpreted with caution.

Tight fitting lids covering squat holes

It is difficult to suggest a causal link between the presence of lids and insect/odour nuisance given the multitude of variables which may affect user perception of nuisance (for example, the fact that in Mozambique there is no containment of insects / odour because the superstructures are not enclosed). However, where lids were recorded (in 345 cases), the trend is towards few cases of either 'strong' smell or large numbers of insects (either hundred or thousands) being reported. By contrast, where lids were absent (n=39) it was found that just over half of all latrine users recorded 'strong smell', and a quarter recorded 'hundreds' of insects. **[ref:simpit:29-32]** Just under two thirds of all cases reported lids 'not damaged' (61%); 37% 'partly chipped' and 2% 'badly broken'. For cases where lids were 'not damaged' or 'partly chipped', the largest percentages were found amongst those categories indicating no or low insect and odour nuisance levels (for example, 'no' or 'slight' smell, 'none' or 'tens' of insects). **[ref:simpit:33-34]**

Table 6: Incidence of insect nuisance by latrine type

Latrine type	Cases	Insect nuisance (% of cases)			
		None	Tens	Hundreds	Thousands
Bucket/pan	194	20	68	10	3
Simple pits	378	46	46	8	1
VIP	30	40	50	3	7
Pour flush	386	71	24	5	0
WC to septic tank	127	79	21	0	0
All latrine types		54	38	6	1

Incidence of insect nuisance by latrine type

The figures for insect nuisance largely mirror those for odour. Again, the majority of cases are registered within the 'none' or 'tens' categories (92% of all cases); bucket/pan latrines show the highest nuisance scores, while water seal latrine types show the lowest nuisance scores (see table 6 above). VIP latrines record the highest rating amongst all latrine types in the 'thousands' category. Factors leading to increased light levels within the VIP latrine superstructure (such as small windows) may help to explain this poor rating.

The findings from the quantitative testing for numbers of insects contained with latrine superstructures tend to reinforce the results from the household survey about insect nuisance [ref:insect:1]. Just over two thirds of all cases sampled (n=71) recorded 0-5 insects, a further 27% cases recorded 6-50 flies, and only 7% recorded 51-100+ insects.

Latrines the primary source of insect nuisance on the household plot?

Anecdotal evidence from interviews with householders about the source of insect nuisance, especially with regard to flies, indicates that the latrine structure is not necessarily the primary source of insect nuisance on the plot. Other important sources include solid waste pits and lane side drains, which when full or blocked, quickly attract flies.

Absence of household latrines

Key findings

- A key reason for the lack of household latrines is poverty, rather than lack of available space on-plot. Poverty, and/or the inability to save funds to invest in longer term sanitation facilities are key constraints

- The relationship between cost, technology choice and income level is a complex one, which defies simple categorisation. There is some evidence to suggest grouping of unskilled employment for those households without sanitation, although this does not remain consistent for lower cost latrine types. Similarly, skilled sources of employment are not the sole source of employment with higher cost latrine types. Choices about sanitary technology are based on a variety of factors, of which cost is just one (important) consideration

---

Background

In the urban context, the factors which determine whether sanitation facilities are present or absent from the household plot are diverse, including issues such as poverty, cost of technology, available space, indebtedness and problems with operation and maintenance. Available literature emphasises the importance of the lack of space in the urban environment as a key feature explaining absence of household sanitation.

Plot size a determinant of absence of household latrine

As mentioned on page 82, criticism of pit latrines focuses on their supposed inappropriateness for small plot sizes. Results from the household survey indicate that for the users, absence of a household latrine is more a function of poverty than available space on the plot. When answering the question, '*Why is there no household toilet?*', the single largest responses from users recorded 'high cost'; and 'use public latrines', factors directly or indirectly linked to income. 'Lack of space' figured only as the third most important response. Poverty may lead householders to prioritise the use of what space they have on plot to other functions, not consistent with sanitation.

Figures from the postal survey of sector professionals tend to reinforce these findings, with cost being cited as the single most significant factor. Combinations of cost and lack of space are also frequently noted. **[ref:post:4]**

Relationship between cost, technology choice and income level

Table 7 shows the outcome when sources of household income are disaggre-

88

Rank	Septic tank	VIP	Pour flush	Simple pit	Bucket	Absent
			Latrine type			
1	Trader	Trader	Labourer	Labourer	Trader	Trader
2	Labourer	Clerk	Mechanic	Trader	Unemployed	Labourer
3	Retired	Retired	Trader	Clerk	Retired	Fisherman
4	Civil servant Clerk Mechanic	Civil servant	Civil servant	Civil servant	Clerk	Unemployed
5	Unemployed	Student	Rail employee	Mechanic	Seamstress	Mechanic

gated by technology type and ranked in order of sample size. Rather than asking the monetary value of a householders income, which would have introduced sampling bias to the results, proxy indicators of income levels were used, in this case, the main source (or profession) which accounted for household income. It is possible to group these professions by type, such as unskilled, semi-skilled and skilled and in this way reach a better idea of the relationship between cost, technology choice and income. Intuitively, it could be argued that given the higher capital costs of particular latrines types (i.e., septic tanks and VIP's), there will be a general trend towards higher income sources of employment being associated with those technology types. Conversely, those households without latrines, or latrines with lowest capital costs, would be assumed to draw on unskilled sources of employment.

What the figures above show is that the situation is much more complex than anticipated. What is observable is that for those households which have no sanitation facility, there is a significant grouping of unskilled jobs which form the basis of household income. This tends to reinforce the findings from the household survey that poverty is one of the key reasons for absence of domestic sanitation. However, the same cannot be said for lower cost types such as bucket/pan latrines or simple pits which have a mix of both unskilled, and skilled sources of employment. Although some grouping of employment types can be identified amongst septic tanks and VIP latrines, the mix of sources is clearly apparent.

This would tend to indicate that there is no strong relationship between cost, technology choice and income, and that technology choice is influenced much more by other factors, such as socio-cultural features. It is also implicit that the householders were able to exercise a choice over their technology, which previous sections (Section B) have shown not necessarily to be the case.

Unsupported initiatives

Examples of households which have provided sanitation facilities outside of existing latrine building programmes are informative in that they may indicate reasons for failure to adopt the programme or highlight particular constraints to potential users of those systems. Householders perceptions about sanitation programmes are critical factors to note. Case study work points to the importance that householders attach to maintaining choice and quality of the latrine type they use (see case study 14 below), despite additional cost considerations to the householder.

Case study 14: Example of unsupported initiative for sanitation provision

---

District: *Ranigaratoth*
City: *Vijayawada, India*
Family size: *4 adults, 2 children*
Income earners: *3 (Husband Rs. 50- per day)*
Occupation: *Labourer/vegetable vendor*

Notes: This family had been previously relocated from an old bustan site to this district. They had built their own home and provided many of their own services with only limited government assistance. They decided to construct their own latrine (outside of the Municipality's low cost sanitation programme) because they perceived problems with the programme's toilets, and did not want to wait for a new latrine construction programme before being able to use their own facility.

The family perceived that the key disadvantage with the programme's toilets was the need for regular pit emptying, so they constructed a [deep] pour-flush single pit. This facility was built at a time when other construction work was on-going, so exact costs were unavailable - however, in conversation with the householders it was estimated that the total cost (including labour) was Rs 5000. A small contractor was employed to build the latrine, and the family

90

saved money from their joint incomes to build the facility. For ten years prior to having a household toilet, the family had resorted to open defecation at a point approximately 200 metres distant. The principal catalyst for latrine construction had been the comfort and convenience it would provide for the users.

User satisfaction

Key findings

* Householders decisions to invest in domestic sanitation are typically driven by socio-cultural rather than health factors

* In all but one case, users express high degrees of satisfaction with their latrine (in excess of 80% recording 'satisfied' or 'very satisfied'). Bucket/pan latrines record by far the highest levels of dissatisfaction

* Many users do not perceive there to be a problem with their latrine. Where problems are recorded, the most common include 'emptying', 'smell' and 'insects', although absolute figures are low

* Of these three problems, 'emptying' and 'smell' have the most impact on satisfaction levels and ability for the user to use the latrine

---

Background
There is little available literature on user perceptions of latrine operation in urban areas, or on changes in attitude caused by problems with operation and maintenance.

Perceived user benefits of sanitation
As a proxy indicator of perceived benefits of sanitation, the household survey asked each family, '*Why did you build a toilet on your plot?*'. The results tend to reinforce the finding that socio-cultural, rather than health factors dominate user decisions to invest in domestic sanitation facilities. Factors including 'comfort and convenience' and 'privacy' account for just under half of all responses (48%). 'Health' accounts for 11%, and other significant minorities include 'government sponsored' (8%), 'no/poor public facilities' (5%) and a combination of comfort/convenience and privacy (5%) **[ref:all:5]**

Expressed levels of user satisfaction
Table 8 shows the aggregated responses to the question, '*How satisfied are*

Table 8: Levels of expressed user satisfaction by technology type

Type	Levels of user satisfaction (% of cases)				
	Very satisfied	Satisfied	Neither	Unsatisfied	Very unsatisfied
Bucket/pan	4	29	19	44	4
Simple pit	22	68	3	6	1
VIP	17	67	6	8	2
Pour flush	10	73	4	8	5
WC septic tank	22	68	3	4	3

you with your toilet?'. The results indicate high levels of expressed satisfaction (83% or more recording 'very satisfied' or 'satisfied') for five of the six latrine types listed. Only bucket/pan latrines show significant levels of dissatisfaction, with just under half of all cases listed as 'unsatisfied' or 'very dissatisfied'.

Problems with operation and maintenance of latrines
In response to the question, *'What problems do you have with your toilet?'*, it was significant that in over half of all cases (54%) there were 'no' problems with the latrine. Where problems were recorded, difficulties with 'emptying' were the most commonly noted minority (12%), with 'smell' and 'insects' recording 7% and 4% respectively. **[ref:all:4]**

Table 9: Most commonly noted problems with latrine by technology type

Type	Problems with latrine (% cases)						
	None	Smell	Insects	Emptying	Repairs	Blockage	Lack water
Bucket/pan	20	4	1	42	–	–	–
Simple pit	73	7	2	1	7	–	–
VIP	52	4	6	8	–	4	–
Pour flush	59	12	8	4	2	5	–
WC septic tank	54	3	5	12	1	5	12
All	54	7	4	12	3	3	2

Table 9 carries a comparison of the most frequently noted problems by technology type. This table reflects the overall picture noted above. An important aspect to note is the high percentages recorded under 'none' for five of the six latrine types tested, with only bucket/pan latrine types recording less than 50% in this category. Additionally, the percentages recorded for smell and insects are relatively small, as compared against those recorded for emptying.

When examining individual technology types several points of interest are observable:

- Simple pit latrines record the highest percentage figures of all types under the 'none' category; and VIP latrines record the second lowest;
- That pour-flush latrines, even with their waterseal, record insects and odours as amongst the most commonly noted problems. However, only 36% of users perceive this odour nuisance to be greater than 'slight';
- Bucket/pan latrine users frequently record 'emptying' problems;
- 'Lack of water' is only mentioned in relation to WC to septic tanks.

What the above comparison does provide is an indication of the relative problems experienced by users of individual technology types, but what is not clear is the impact that these problems have on the user's satisfaction of their latrines. Crosstabulations between these two variables are informative in that they indicate which of the above problems have the strongest impact on satisfaction levels. Examining the percentage of cases that fall in the two most dissatisfied categories (see Table 10) indicates that of the six most

Table 10: Crosstabulations between recorded problems and user satisfaction

Problem	% of all cases				
	Very unsatisfied	Unsatisfied	Neither	Satisfied	Very satisfied
Smell	0.3	1.6	0.6	4.5	0.2
Insects	0.1	0.1	0.1	3.7	0.3
Emptying	0.1	4.6	2.1	4.6	0.6
Repairs	0.1	0.3	0.1	1.8	0.5
Blockage	0.1	0.4	0.4	1.5	0.3
Lack water	0.2	0.5	0	0.9	0.3

Table 11: Crosstabulations between recorded problems and perceived impact on use of latrine

Problem	Impact on use of latrine (% of all cases)				
	No impact	Slight impact	Moderate impact	Strong impact	Cannot continue to use
Smell	3.7	2.5	0.4	0.5	0.4
Insects	3.7	0.5	0.2	0	0.1
Emptying	1.8	5.4	2.1	2.1	0.6
Repairs	0.7	1.7	0.4	0.1	0.1
Blockage	0.3	1.6	0.1	0.1	0.7
Lack water	0.1	1.3	0.3	0.2	0

prominent problems listed in Table 9, only 'emptying' and 'smell' impact significantly on dissatisfaction levels (defined here as larger than 1.0% of all cases).

Crosstabulations between recorded problems and their perceived impact on continued use of the household latrine reinforces this point. Of the problems identified, only 'emptying' and 'smell' account for a cumulative figure of more than 1% of all cases in the three categories indicating more than a moderate impact on continued use of the latrine, as table 11 illustrates.

94

Latrine emptying

Key findings

- Manual methods of emptying dominate, and are especially commonplace for simple pit and pour flush latrines. As expected, mechanical emptying tends to be associated with VIP and septic tank latrines

- The responsibility for emptying latrines is normally either that of the users, or contractors. Contractors are of particular importance in the emptying of bucket/pan and pour flush latrines

- For those latrines which had been emptied, most had been used for 6, 7, or 8 years. Typically, these latrines had been emptied either once or twice

- Rates for re-filling of previously emptied latrines indicate that the majority fill over 3-6 years

- Where users expressed a problem with emptying, frequency, cost and hygiene were ranked as the three most important issues

- In the majority of cases, the final disposal site for collected excreta was either unknown or indiscriminate dumping

---

Background
When pit latrines or septic tanks become full, they must be either taken out of use and a new pit dug, or the pit/tank emptied. The practice of emptying pits by hand can present serious health hazards if the faecal matter has not been rested for at least two years. Where suitable equipment is available, lined pits can be mechanically emptied, although there are serious limitations presented by densely crowded urban areas and access to plots and the cost involved in using vacuum tankers.

How latrines are emptied
Results from the household survey indicate that where latrines are emptied, the most common practice is for manual emptying either by hand or with handtools. In response to the question, *'How is the pit / tank emptied?'*, just over one third (37%) of all households employed manual forms of emptying, with only 9% favouring vacuum tankers. Significantly, just over half of all responses (53%) replied that the household latrine had not been emptied. **[ref:all:6]**

Which types of latrines are emptied by what method?
Table 12 compares latrine type by emptying method. The results tend to confirm that for bucket/pan, simple pit and pour-flush latrine types that

Table 12: Comparison of latrine types and emptying method

Type	Emptying method (% of cases)				
	Manually by hand	Manually with handtools	Vacuum tanker	Other methods	Not emptied
Bucket/pan	100	–	–	–	–
Simple pit	6	1	4	1	87
VIP	2	25	35	4	35
Pour flush	14	21	–	–	64
WC septic tank	7	5	50	–	37

manual emptying methods dominate. The large percentage figure recorded for vacuum tankers under WC to septic tanks is to be expected. Interestingly, the relatively low percentage figures for 'not emptied' suggest a more frequent emptying rate for VIP's and WC's to septic tanks as compared to other latrine types, a fact borne out in the analysis of re-emptying rates.

Who does the emptying?

If manual methods tend to dominate latrine emptying, who actually empties the pit/tank, and who pays? The household survey asked the question, *'Who is responsible for emptying the pit/tank?'* and the general findings show that users were normally those responsible for this process (45%), with contractors and the municipality recording 35% and 18% respectively. **[ref:all:7]**

There is significant variation by type however, as table 13 below illustrates. Unsurprisingly, the bucket/pan system records the highest figures for the use of a contractor, normally an individual drawn from the informal sector. The use of contractors for emptying in this case may be a legacy of the era in which a formalised system of emptying was in place with conservancy labourers removing nightsoil daily.

Two points of clarification are required in explaining table 13. Although a high percentage figure was recorded for 'user' in relation to emptying of pour-flush latrines, experience from India suggests that given the prevailing cultural taboo associated with handling faecal matter, almost all responsibility for emptying is that of contractors, typically 'scavengers'. Such a discrepancy may have arisen from the local translation of 'responsibility'

96

Table 13: Responsibility for emptying by latrine type

	% of all cases		
Type	User	Contractor	Municipality
Bucket/pan	29	63	8
Simple pit	67	19	14
VIP	20	26	54
Pour flush	81	12	8
WC septic tank	29	19	51

into Telegu. Secondly, to some extent this table may reflect the perceptions of householders as to who is responsible, rather than who actually performs the task of emptying. For instance, the responses for 'municipality' in relation to simple pit latrines and pour-flush latrines are not consistent with actual practice.

Length of time latrine in use
The length of time a latrine has been used by a household and the frequency with which it has been emptied is an important indicator of its performance and sustainability. For those latrines which were recorded as 'not emptied' from the household survey, breakdown of figures reveals that just under 60% had been used for between 1-10 years (with 40% falling in the 1-5 year category; 18% in the 6-10 year category).

Selected year by year breakdown is shown in table 14, and indicates a significant skewing towards years 1-3.

In those cases where latrines had been emptied, the majority (88%) had been emptied between 1-6 times. Of these, most latrines had been emptied either

Table 14: Breakdown of number of years latrine in use recorded as not emptied (selected years: 1-10; excluding bucket/pan latrine)

	Years in use (% of all cases)									
	1	2	3	4	5	6	7	8	9	10
Not emptied	11.8	9.8	8.9	5.3	4.1	4.9	5.4	2.8	1.8	3.2

Table 15: Breakdown of years latrines used by number of times emptied (excluding bucket/pan latrines)

Times emptied	Years in use (% of all cases)										
	1	2	3	4	5	6	7	8	9	10	Total
1	1.5	3.0	1.5	2.0	3.0	4.5	6.5	6.0	1.5	5.0	34.5
2			1.0	2.0	2.0	2.5	2.0	2.0		1.0	12.5
3	0.5		1.5	1.0	0.5	0.5	1.0	1.5		0.5	7.0
4			0.5	0.5		1.0	0.5				2.5
5			0.5								0.5
6		0.5	0.5			1.0			0.5	0.5	3.0
Total	2.0	3.5	5.5	5.5	5.5	9.5	10	9.5	2.0	7.0	

once or twice, with most being used for between 6-8 years (see table 15 above). These figures question the assumptions made about the high frequency of latrine emptying in low income urban areas and the short time period between initial use and first emptying.

Re-emptying periods

Householders were asked, *'How long does it take for the pit/tank to require emptying again?'*. The responses are indicative of the rate at which a recently emptied pit/tank fills again. Professionals assumptions in this area tend towards short re-emptying periods. However, this research indicates that for both simple pit and pour-flush latrine types longer refilling periods (typically

Table 16: Breakdown of re-emptying period by latrine type (excluding bucket/pan latrines)

	Time taken for pit to refill (m = months / y = years) % of cases								
	3m	4m	6m	1 yr	2 yr	3-4 yr	5-6 yr	7-9 yr	10-11 yr
Simple pit	3	6	12	13	7	22	19	4	8
VIP	–	–	42	21	21	8	4	–	4
Pour flush	–	–	1	10	21	32	27	–	–
WC septic tank	9	3	23	13	19	30	4	–	–
All	3	2	7	6	8	12	8	1	2

3-4 and 5-6 years) are commonplace, whereas VIP and WC to septic tank types record larger percentages in the 6 months, 1 and 2 year categories (See table 16).

When examining the combined figures for all latrines, there are two points to note: the 20% of all latrines emptied with refill periods of between 3-6 years, and the relatively high proportion of all latrines recording refill rates of every 6 months, 1 or 2 years (21%). These latter figures may well be skewed by the impact of both VIP and WC to septic tank latrine types recording relatively large percentages between the 6 months - 2 years categories.

Problems with emptying
An earlier section of this report has already noted that 'emptying' constituted the single most common problem noted with all latrine types (see page 92 and table 9) and was one issue which significantly affected user satisfaction of latrines (see page 92 and table 8). Paradoxically, when householders were asked, *'What problems do you have with pit/tank emptying?'*, 45% of all cases recorded 'none'. Where problems were noted, the most significant issues included 'frequency', 'high cost' and 'hygiene'. Other factors which might have been assumed to have been of importance, such as 'access to plot' or 'odour', recorded only 3% and 0.5% of all cases respectively.

A clearer picture of why 'frequency' heads this list is seen in the table below, comparing latrine type with emptying problem. The frequency of emptying for bucket/pan latrines is clearly the most significant factor for this type and skews the overall figures as a result. It is clear that the cost of emptying is a

Table 17: Type of emptying problem by latrine type						
	% of all cases					
	High cost	Frequency	Hygiene	Access	None	Others
Bucket/pan	9	46	3	–	38	5
Simple pit	28	17	–	3	50	2
VIP	45	–	–	–	45	10
Pour flush	29	5	14	4	46	2
WC septic tank	12	5	1	11	60	11
All	19	21	6	3	45	

key problem more consistently noted by all latrine types, particularly with regard to the VIP, pour flush and simple pit latrines.

Disposal of pit contents following emptying
The final destination of emptied pit excreta and its disposal method is critical to maintenance of a community's health. As a means to establishing empty-ing outcomes, the household survey asked, *'What happens to the contents of the pit/tank after emptying?'*. The figures tend to show that in the majority of cases the final destination of pit excreta is 'indiscriminate dumping' or 'unknown' (accounting for 34% and 33% of all cases respectively). A significant minority (24%) reported that pit contents were disposed of hygienically off-site (though few householders could say where these site were), and only 8% replied that contents were buried on-plot. **[ref:all:7]**

Double pit latrines

Key findings
* Need for more frequent user support and education activities to be made available

* Construction related problems were infrequently noted by users. Of greater concern were correct operation and maintenance of twin and double pit latrines

---

Background
There are occasions when two shallow pits may be more appropriate than a single deep pit, such as in cases where the underlying geology of an area is difficult to excavate, or where groundwater levels are within one or two metres of the surface. In alternating double pits, accumulated solids in one pit are left for a 'safe' period until the excreta has decomposed and can be handled without health risk. During the resting period, the alternative pit is used by the household. Where separate twin pits are used as with pour-flush latrines, a Y-junction and access chamber are constructed to allow the users to direct excreta from one pit to another.

Concern about twin and double pits has focused on construction related and operational problems. For correct operation of double pit offset pour-flush latrines, for example, particular care has to be taken with the construction of the Y-junction, and the user must be made aware of how the latrine should be operated. Longer term support facilities, training and demonstration of operation are key elements to operational success.

Construction related problems

This research indicates the primacy of operation and maintenance, over construction related problems with this latrine type. The household survey found that users of twin or double pit latrines did not rank construction related problems as a key concern. The most relevant construction related problem, 'blockages', accounted for only a minority of cases for both pour-flush twin pit latrines (5%) and double VIP latrines (4%).

Although drawn from an admittedly small sample (n=57), postal survey results tend to confirm this point, showing that 'construction related' problems accounted for only 3% of all problems found amongst double pits. Of much greater significance were factors relating to the correct operation and maintenance of double pits, including both pits being used at the same time / pits not rested (28% of all problems). **[ref.:post:3]**

Some anecdotal evidence during fieldwork indicated that the blockages recorded in some double pit latrines were attributable to the use of high density plastic (HDP) pans which were not as efficient at transporting flushed excreta as ceramic pans.

Inadequacy of education and support for users

The key position of operation and maintenance related problems points to the need for a more effective and sustained procedure of user education and support. Although in the programmes studied for this research, householders were given a practical demonstration of how the pour-flush latrine works, how to recognise when a pit is full and the method to alternate from one pit to another, this failed to address a wider problem that the existing procedure of demonstrating latrine operation had been tied to the masons who originally constructed the latrines. When new owners or tenants moved onto the plot, no framework for provision of guidance was available. Training and support for scavengers on latrine use may help to mitigate this problem.

Groundwater pollution

Key findings

* Determining the movement of viruses and bacteria in soils is extremely difficult, and involves a complex interaction of soil profile and hydraulic conductivity parameters, temperature, soil pH, moisture retention capacity. The clay content of the unsaturated zone is amongst the single most important indicator of the likely mobility of contaminants and its subsequent impact on groundwater pollution

* Larger sized contaminants (helminths and protozoa) are normally effectively removed by physical filtration; bacteria are normally filtered by clayey soils. Of most concern are waterborne viruses which are too small for even fine grained clays to filter

* Viruses *normally* die-off within three metres of the pollution source, irrespective of soil type. Bacterial contamination is *normally* removed given sufficient depth of unsaturated soil (at least 2 metres) between the pollution source and water point. A minimum distance of 15 metres between a pollution source and a downstream water point is sufficient for removal of all contaminants

* Health risks associated with groundwater pollution should be set against the much greater hazard of open defecation. The potential for groundwater pollution from pit latrine systems should not be used as the sole argument for not installing these systems

Background

A problem that is noted in relation to on-plot sanitation is the potential for pollution of groundwater that is associated with these systems. Contamination from on-plot systems can be categorised as follows:

Microbiological contaminants: liquids percolating into the soil from latrine pits or septic tanks contain large numbers of micro-organisms of faecal origin, including viruses, bacteria, protozoa and helminths.

Chemical contaminants: including nitrogen and phosphorus. Chemical pollution extends much further than pollution by micro-organisms. In areas with high pit latrine densities, nitrate concentrations may build up to in excess of World Health Organisation (WHO) drinking water guidelines. The main health hazard in such an event is 'blue baby syndrome' or methaemoglobinaemia, when milk powder is mixed with contaminated water and fed to young infants. If left untreated, this can prove fatal.

Thus, groundwater under or near pit latrines may become polluted which can be a serious problem when it affects the quality of drinking water drawn from wells and boreholes. Water in leaky pipes may also be contaminated if the pressure drops and polluted groundwater levels are above the pipes.

A particular problem in densely populated urban areas is the possible proximity of latrine pits and shallow wells on neighbouring plots. Whilst the levels of service for water supply remain poor, many urban dwellers are likely to use a nearby shallow well if the groundwater table is sufficiently high. The lack of effective urban development planning control means that it is very difficult to regulate and enforce the relative location of latrines and wells on plots, even in formally developed areas.

All types of sanitation pose a pollution threat of some kind. Fourie and Ryneveld (1995) argue that when considering pollution from on-plot sanitation, there are three primary aspects to consider:

1. That human excreta contains a number of different possible contaminants
2. That at sufficiently high doses, these contaminants are potentially hazardous to human health and or the natural environment
3. In order for a dose to be transmitted to a host, the contaminants must be sent by one route or another from the source to individuals or to the environment

A key route to transmission is the subsurface, hence a clear understanding of contaminant movement and the factors which affect it is critical to the development of guidelines for minimising pollution risk to groundwater sources from these sanitation systems.

Literature review: key points

General contaminant movement
- On reaching the groundwater table, the rate of contaminant movement will be much greater than in the unsaturated zone, and this movement will be in the direction of the regional groundwater flow;
- The presence of macropores in the soil (caused by channels formed from decomposed roots, or rock fissures) may significantly increase contaminant movement;
- Studies by Sengupta (1996) indicate that contaminant travel is higher in sandy soils than in clayey silt or silty clay soils;
- An understanding of the physical and chemical processes that remove

103

contaminants from water during movement through the subsurface is important in understanding whether influent from a particular latrine will pollute a drinking water source;

- The movement of contaminants through the subsurface is affected by processes which may affect the concentration and composition of the contaminants;
- It is unclear to what extent nitrate can be denitrified in the soil to produce nitrogen gas which will escape into the atmosphere.

Microbiological contamination

- The mobility of the four principal microbiological organisms (viruses, bacteria, protozoa and helminths) is affected by both their physical size and chemical/other processes.
- Larger sized contaminants (helminths and protozoa) are normally effectively removed by physical filtration by soil adjacent and below the pollution source; bacteria are normally filtered by clayey soils. Of most concern are waterborne viruses which are too small for even fine grained clays to filter. Effective physical filtration is highly dependent on the particle size of the soil, with well-graded soil being the most effective filter.
- Chemical processes such as adsorption (whereby foreign bodies become attached to the surface of the soil, thus reducing the free energy of the surface) are critical to effective virus removal in the subsurface region, and tends to be most effective where pH levels are low (Stumm & Morgan, 1981). Since adsorption is unlikely in already saturated soils, maximising residence times in unsaturated zones is a key factor to removal and elimination of these viruses.
- Adsorption of viruses is considered most effective in clayey soils (Drewry and Eliassen, 1968; Tim and Mostaghimi, 1991).

Chemical contamination

The contaminants of most importance in this category are nitrates and phosphates. The latter are removed by adsorption by almost all soil types (excluding coarse, clean gravels) within a short distance from the pollution source.

- The removal of nitrates in the subsurface is dependent primarily on microbiological rather than physical processes.

Hydrogeological factors affecting movement of contaminants

* The permeability of a soil between a pit and the groundwater level is a key factor in determining the possible contamination of groundwater from such sources.
* Not all soil profiles are uniform; most are heterogeneous, and may have different hydraulic conductivities in both vertical and horizontal directions.
* There is significant difference of opinion between sector professionals as to what constitutes the ideal soil for minimising contamination from on-plot sanitation facilities. Some (Romero, 1972; Fekpe et al, 1992) express a preference for free-draining soils (such as coarse sands). This conflicts with other researchers (Taussig and Connelly, 1991; Lewis et al, 1980) who argue that fine, graded soils, with a thickness of 2-3 metres, and clays, are more suitable.
* Subsurface flow of water is significantly affected by the presence of macropores in the soil profiles. Highly fractured bedrock close to, or at the soil surface, for instance, will facilitate contaminant movement to groundwater levels.

Movement of viruses, bacteria and nitrates

* For viruses, the bulk of existing literature indicates almost complete die-off within three metres of the pollution source, irrespective of soil type. In a study by Gerba et al, 1975, all but one virus type indicated travel distances for viruses of less than one metre. Lower rates of virus removal are achieved in coarser soils. In fast flowing groundwater conditions however, pollution may travel up to 25 metres (Caldwell, 1937).
* With bacterial contamination, existing literature indicates that given sufficient depth of intact, unsaturated soil between the source of contamination and the groundwater, virtually all bacterial pollution should be removed. There is general consensus that 'sufficient depth' implies two metres, as long as the rate of effluent application does not exceed 50mm/day. In locations with intense rainfall, this distance may need to be increased as higher infiltration rates may carry polluted water further through the subsurface.
* It is generally agreed that a minimum distance of 15 metres between a pollution source and a downstream water point is satisfactory for the removal of contaminants.
* Determination of nitrate pollution should proceed from an initial assessment of background nitrate levels, since contamination can be derived

from a number of sources other than on-plot sanitation systems.
* Literature indicates that the key condition for minimising nitrate contamination of groundwater is to maximise its residence time in the unsaturated zone, which has a smaller hydraulic conductivity than the saturated zone and hence delays the time at which nitrates enter the saturated zone. Studies by Cochet et al, 1990 and Sikora and Keeney, 1976, suggest that it may be possible to alter the conditions of the unsaturated zone to some extent, increasing denitrification processes by adding carbon either to the soil surrounding the pit or soakaway, or the influent itself.

Relative health risks

The issue of groundwater pollution is essentially one of weighing relative health risks. The contamination of the surface environment through open defecation is the primary environmental concern since this has the greatest potential to transmit health hazards to the wider community. There are obviously health risks associated with groundwater pollution when communities are abstracting water from nearby shallow wells for domestic consumption, but these risks need to be viewed in perspective to the risks from faecal contamination at the ground surface.

Local solutions

Cotton (1997) argues that groundwater pollution can be dealt with in two ways: modifications to the sanitation system (i.e., soakpit surrounded by sand envelope), or through changes to the water supply system (i.e., establishing a reticulation system with standposts to reduce the need for using groundwater for domestic consumption). Other options for consideration include extracting water from a lower level in the aquifer, which is acceptable assuming low extraction rates and proper sealing of well casings as it passes through the pollution zone.

Section 2B
Sample characteristics (by technology type)

Absence of household latrine

Main points include:

- With regard to tenure status, there was an even split between tenants (45%) and landlords (52%). 3% of all cases defined as 'caretaker'.
- The number of people on-plot ranged between a minimum of 1, and a maximum of 94, the latter accounting for cases where several families reside within the same plot, typically in compound housing. The arithmetic mean figured at 17, the median figure is 14 and the mode 10.
- Of those cases where a response was provided (in 57% of cases), the majority (97%) claimed that no members of the household currently had diarrhoea.
- In just under one third of all cases (32%), no consumer items (defined as television, radio, iron, refrigerator, or other electrical goods) were identified by surveyors. The single most popular item, a radio, was found in 15% of cases, and in 27% both a radio and television were recorded. Households in which three or more consumer items were identified accounted for 21% of all cases.
- Household plot size (m^2) varied in range from a minimum of $11m^2$ to a maximum of $2700m^2$. The arithmetic mean figured at $466m^2$, with a median figure of $432m^2$ and a mode of $630m^2$.

Bucket/pan latrine

Main points include:

- Tenure status of households with bucket/pan latrines indicates that 46% are tenants and 53% are owners. 1% of all cases defined as 'caretaker'.
- Number of people on-plot ranges from a minimum of 1, to a maximum of 300. The mean number of individuals on-plot is 19, the median figure is 16 and the mode 15.
- In those cases where a response was provided (61%), 95% claimed that no members of the household currently had diarrhoea; 3% of cases recorded one individual with diarrhoea; 2% with two household members.
- The mean number of adults using bucket/pan latrines is 11; the maximum 38. Largest percentages were recorded amongst households with 8, 9 or

107

10 adults.
- In only 9% of all cases were households found to have no consumer items. A radio and television were the single most commonly recorded item (37%); a radio was identified in 13% of cases. Households in which 3 or more consumer items were identified accounted for 38% of all cases.
- 89% of all cases indicate a lid to bucket/pan is present (as a way of reducing odour and insect nuisance). In 91% of cases this lid was undamaged, forming a sound seal; the remaining 9% of cases were partly damaged, or chipped.
- Mean latrine superstructure size (m^2) is 2.5m^2; median - 2.0m^2 and mode, 2.0m^2

Simple pit latrines

- Tenure status of households with simple pit latrines indicate that 31% are tenants and 64% are owners. 4% of all cases defined as 'caretaker'.
- Number of people on-plot ranges from a minimum of 1, to a maximum of 100. The mean number of individuals on-plot is 8, the median figure is 7 and the mode 6.
- In those cases where a response was provided (23%), 80% claimed that no members of the household currently had diarrhoea; 18% of cases recorded one individual with diarrhoea.
- The mean number of adults using simple pit latrines is 5; the maximum 33. Largest percentages found amongst households with 3, 4 or 5 adults.
- In one-third of all cases, households were found to have no consumer items. Radios were the single most commonly recorded item (47%); a radio and television were recorded in 17% of cases. Households in which three or more consumer items were identified accounted for 19% of all cases.
- 85% of all simple pits were estimated to have pit depth of between 3-6 feet; 11% 7-10 feet and 4% 11 feet and deeper. The deepest pit recorded was 23 feet. Crosstabulations between depth of pit and users perception of smell failed to prove any statistically significant relationship between the two variables.
- 90% of all cases indicate a lid to the pit is present (as a way of reducing odour and insect nuisance). In just under two-thirds of all cases, this lid was undamaged, forming a sound seal; in 37% of cases the lid was partly damaged, or chipped, and in 1.5% the lid was badly broken. Crosstabulations between presence of lids to toilets and users perception of odour indicate a fall in cases between 'no smell' (52%) and 'strong smell' (4%).
- Mean shelter size (m^2) is 6.6m^2; median - 6.0m^2 and mode, 6.0m^2.

Ventilated Improved Pit (VIP) latrines

- Tenure status of households with ventilated improved pit latrines indicate that 33% are tenants and 67% are owners.
- Number of people on-plot ranges from a minimum of 1, to a maximum of 120. The mean number of individuals on-plot is 19, the median 15 and the mode 10.
- In those cases where a response was provided (57%), all claimed that no members of the household currently had diarrhoea.
- The mean number of adults using VIP latrines is 11; the maximum 90. Largest percentages found amongst households with 5, 6, 7 or 10 adults.
- 15% of households were found to have no consumer items. 66% of households possessed both radio and television. Households in which 3 or more consumer items were identified accounted for 9% of all cases.
- 24% of all VIP latrines were estimated to have pit depth of between 4-6 feet; 68% 7-10 feet and 8% 11 feet and deeper. The deepest pit recorded was 28 feet.
- Mean shelter size (m²) is 3.3m²; median - 2.3m² and mode, 1.8m².

Pour-flush latrines

- The sample shows that 95% of households were identified as owners, with only 5% tenants.
- Number of people on-plot ranges from a minimum of 2, to a maximum of 20. The mean number of individuals on-plot is 8, the median 7 and the mode 5.
- In those cases where a response was provided (68%), 99% claimed that no members of the household currently had diarrhoea.
- The mean number of adults using pour flush latrines is 5; the maximum 20. Largest percentages found amongst households with 2-6 adults.
- 38% of households were found to have no consumer items. 28% of households possessed a television, 23% both radio and television and 10% a radio.
- 73% of all pour flush latrines were estimated to have pit depth of between 4-6 feet; 20% 7-10 feet and 5% 11 feet and deeper. The deepest pit recorded was 13 feet.
- Mean shelter size (m²) is 1.5m²; median - 1.0m² and mode, 1.0 m².

WC to septic tanks

- The sample shows that 54% of households were identified as owners, 44% as tenants and 1% as caretaker.
- Number of people on-plot ranges from a minimum of 1, to a maximum of

80. The mean number of individuals on-plot is 12, the median 9 and the mode 4.

- In those cases where a response was provided (57%), 99% claimed that no members of the household currently had diarrhoea.
- The mean number of adults using WC to septic tanks is 9; the maximum 65. Largest percentages found amongst households with 3, 4, 5 and 6 adults.
- A relatively small 15% of households were found to have no consumer items. 28% of households possessed a television and radio; and households in which 3 or more consumer items were identified accounted for 43% of all cases.
- Mean shelter size (m^2) is 2.1m^2; median - 2.1m^2 and mode, 1.8 m^2.

Section 2C
Database listing

Full copies of all data output referenced in this report can be obtained from the project authors.

This includes:
- Data output based on household surveys, postal surveys and field tests. This information is broken down by latrine type and country;

- Full text versions of semi-structured interviews. These include interview with:

  - MATTHEW ADOMBIRE; Acting Director (Planning and Development), GWSC; Ghana.
  - MARIA DOS ANJOS; Head of WSS department for MoH; Mozambique.
  - F N ARKO; Executive Secretary/Programme Manager, CEDECOM, Cape Coast, Ghana.
  - N A ARMAH; Chief Mechanical Engineer, Waste Management Department, Accra Metropolitan Assembly, Ghana.
  - FRANCIS AWINDAOGO; Regional co-ordinator GWSC, Tamale, Ghana.
  - DAN AYIVIE; Project Manager, Accra Sustainable Programme, Town & Country Planning Dept, Accra, Ghana.
  - EMMANUAL BAWA; Water and Sanitation Officer, UNICEF, Ghana.
  - BEN DOE; Project Manager, Accra Sustainable Programme, Town & Country Planning Dept, Accra, Ghana.
  - ODOUROI DONKOR; Project Officer, ProNet, Accra, Ghana.
  - LUIS ELIAS; Head of National Water Directorate, Maputo, Mozambique.
  - TAMALE SANITARY COMMITTEE OFFICIALS; Tamale, Ghana.
  - JOSE NAENE and HELENA COVANE; animators for Jorge Dimitrov and Urbanicazao districts, Maputo, Mozambique.
  - K RAJENDRA PRASAD; Deputy Executive Engineer, Vijayawada Slum Improvement Project, Vijayawada, India.

111

–   GANGADHARARAO MEKA; Assistant City Planner, Vijayawada
    Slum Improvement Project, Vijayawada, India.

•   Video film of low income urban conditions in Ghana, Mozambique and
    India;

Copies can be provided, on request to:

Darren Saywell
Research Associate
Water, Engineering and Development Centre
Loughborough University
Leicestershire LE11 3TU
UK

Fax: +44 1509 211079
E-mail: WEDC@lboro.ac.uk

Section 2D
Bibliography

The references listed in this section include those documents referred to in this report and a selection of publications from the original literature review which may obtained by professionals in developing countries.

AASEN Barnt and MACRAE Alexander, 1992. The Tegucigalpa model: water and sanitation through community management. *Waterfront*, Issue 1, February, 6

ADHYA A KALL G J, 1989. A permeable lining for seepage pits. *Waterlines*, **8**, 1, July, 30 - 32.

AGARWAL Anil, 1985. Taboos make hygiene difficult for women. *GATE*, No 4, p 29

AHMED Viqar, 1986. Lahore walled city upgrading project. In *Reaching the urban poor* (Ed Cheema). Westview Press, Boulder. Pages 45 - 60.

AKOWUAH E K O, 1985. Experiences and lessons from the operation of Monrovia sewerage system. In *Water and sanitation in Africa*. Proc 11th WEDC Conference, Dar es Salaam, 15 - 19 April 1985. WEDC, Loughborough. Pages 11 - 14

ALAERTS G J, VEENSTRA S, BENTVELSEN M, van DUIJL L A and others, 1991. *Feasibility of anaerobic sewage treatment in sanitation strategies in developing countries*. IHE Report Series 20. International Institute for Hydraulic and Environmental Engineering, Delft.

ALLAN Joseph B, 1995 *Report on household demand for improved sanitation: a case study of selected communities in the Accra metropolitan authority and the Ga rural district* Pronet, Accra

113

ANNAN Akweley, CROMPTON D W T, WALTERS D E and ARNOLD S E (Annan et al), 1986. An investigation of the prevalence of intestinal parasites in pre-school children in Ghana. *Parasitology*, **92**, 209 - 217.

APPLETON Judith, 1987. *Drought relief in Ethiopia: planning and management of feeding programmes: a practical guide*. Save the Children, London.

ASSAR M, 1971. *Guide to sanitation in natural disasters*. World Health Organization, Geneva.

BAKHTEARI, Quratul Ain and WEGELIN-SCHURINGA, Madeleen. (1992). *From sanitation to development, the case of the Baldia soakpit pilot project*. Technical Paper Series 31. IRC, The Hague

BALLHATCHET Kenneth and HARRISON John (Ed), 1980. *The city in South Asia: pre-modern and modern*. Curzon Press, London.

BANGLADESH RURAL WATER SUPPLY AND ENVIRONMENTAL SANITATION PROGRAMME (Bangladesh RWS&ESP), 1983. *User perceptions and observed use of latrines in Rahamaterpara*. Evaluation of Latrine Technology, Volume II. DPHE-UNICEF-WHO, Dhaka.

BARROW Nita, 1981. Knowledge belongs to everyone: the challenge in adult education and primary health care. *Convergence*, **14**, 2, 45 - 52.

BASAAKO Kebadire, PARKER Ronald, WALLER Robert B and WILSON James G (Basaako et al), 1983. *Handbook for district sanitation coordinators*. TAG Technical Note No 9. The World Bank, Washington DC.

BASKARAN T R, 1980. Risk of pollution of water supplies from pit latrines. *Report of the International Seminar on low-cost techniques for disposal of human wastes in urban communities*. Calcutta, February. Annexure VI.

BELLARD Brian, 1981. Financing of low-cost sanitation schemes in the urban areas of Botswana. In *Sanitation in developing countries*. Proceedings of a workshop on training held in Lobatse, Botswana, 14-20 August 1980. IDRC, Ottawa. Pages 131 - 134.

BERRY Andrew, 1993 Bridging the communication gap: social marketing and WATSAN In Franceys, R (ed). *Institutional Development Series: No. 5*, WEDC, Loughborough University

BIELLIK Robin J and HENDERSON Peggy L, 1984. The performance of aquaprivies in Thai refugee camps. *Waterlines*, **3**, 1, July, 22 - 24

BLACKETT Isabel, 1988. Co-ordinating a national sanitation programme: the Lesotho way. *Waterlines*, **6**, 3, January, 12 - 13.

BLACKMORE Michael D, BOYDELL Robert A and MBERE Nomtuse (Blackmore et al), 1978. Choice of technology in Botswana. In *Sanitation in developing countries* (Ed Pacey). John Wiley & Sons, Chichester.

BRADLEY R M, 1983. The choice between septic tanks and sewers in tropical developing countries. *The Public Health Engineer*, **11**, 1, January, 20 - 28.

BRADLEY R M and RAUCHER R L, 1988. A technical and economic comparison of nightsoil and sewerage systems in urban areas. *Water S A*, **14**, 1, January, 49 - 57.

BRANDBERG Bjorn, 1983. *The latrine project, Mozambique*. IDRC-MR58e. International Development Research Centre, Ottawa.

BRANDBERG Bjorn, 1985.Why should a latrine look like a house? *Waterlines*, 3, 3, January,24 26.

BRANDBERG Bjorn, 1991a. The SanPlat system: lowest cost environmental sanitation. In *Infrastructure, environment, water and people*. Proc 17th WEDC Conference, Nairobi, 19 - 23 August. WEDC, Loughborough. Pages 193 - 196.

BRANDBERG Bjorn, 1991b. *Planning, construction and operation of public and institutional latrines*. Hesawa Programme Management, Stockholm.

BRANDBERG B and JEREMIAS M, 1981. Housing sanitation, Mozambique. In *Sanitation in developing countries*. Proceedings of a workshop on training held in Lobatse, Botswana, 14-20 August 1980. IDRC, Ottawa. Pages 21 - 23.

BRISCOE J, FEACHEM R and RAHAMAN M M (Briscoe et al), 1986. *Evaluating health impact: water supply, sanitation and hygiene education.* International Development Research Centre, Ottawa, Canada.

BRITISH STANDARDS INSTITUTION (BSI), 19??. *Design and installation of small sewage treatment works and cesspools.* BSI, London.

BROWN, Ato, 1985. The task of renovation and operation of water supply and sanitation in Ghana. In *Water and sanitation in Africa*. Proc 11th WEDC Conference, Dar es Salaam, 15 - 19 April 1985. WEDC, Loughborough. Pages 15 - 18.

BUREN Ariane van, 1979 (Ed). *A Chinese biogas manual.* Translated from the Chinese by Michael Crook. IT Publications, London.

BUREN Ariane van, McMICHAEL Joan, CACERES Roberto and CACERES Armando (Buren et al), 1984. Composting latrines in Guatemala. *Ambio*, **13**, 4, 274 - 277.

BURGERS Lizette, BOOT Marieke and WIJK-SIJBESMA Christine van, 1988. *Hygiene education in water supply and sanitation programmes: literature review with selected and annotated bibliography.*Technical Paper No 27. IRC, The Hague.

CAIRNCROSS Sandy, 1988. *Small scale sanitation.* Ross Bulletin No 8. The Ross Institute, London.

CAIRNCROSS Sandy, 1989. Water supply and sanitation: an agenda for research. *Journal of Tropical Medicine and Hygiene*, **92**, 301 - 314.

CAIRNCROSS Sandy and FEACHEM Richard G, 1993. *Environmental health engineering in the tropics.* 2nd ed. John Wiley & Sons, Chichester.

CALDWELL EL, 1937 Groundwater pollution and the bored hole latrine. *J. Infect. Dis.* **61** 148-183

CAMPBELL Dan, 1988. Data collection for the design of water and sanitation projects in Belize. *Waterlines*, **6**, 3, January, 26 - 28.

CARROLL R F, 1984. *BREVAC: a mechanised method of emptying sanitary chambers*. IP 1/84. Building Research Establishment, Garston, England.

CARROLL R F, 1985. Mechanised emptying of pit latrines in Africa. In *Water and sanitation in Africa*. Proc 11th WEDC Conference, Dar es Salaam, 15 - 19 April 1985. WEDC, Loughborough. Pages 29 - 32.

CARTER J C, 1938. The bored-hole latrine. *Bulletin of Hygiene*, **13**, 8, August, 591 - 600.

CHADHA Skylark and STRAUSS Martin, 1991. *Promotion of rural sanitation in Bangladesh with private sector participation*. Swiss Development Corporation, Dhaka, Bangladesh.

CHARNOCK Gary, 1983. Patel promotes people participation. *World Water*, **6**, 12, December, 31 - 32.

COCHET et al, 1990 Soil absorption systems and nitrogen removal. *Water Sci. Technol.* 22 (3/4) 109-116

COFFEY Manus, 1988. Low cost latrine emptying vehicle. In *Water and urban services in Asia and the Pacific*. Proceedings of the 14th WEDC Conference, Kuala Lumpur, 11 - 15 April 1988. WEDC, Loughborough. Pages 77 - 80.

COTTON Andrew and FRANCEYS Richard, 1987. Sanitation for rural housing in Sri Lanka. *Waterlines*, **5**, 3, January, 9 - 11.

COTTON A P and FRANCEYS R W A, 1988. Urban infrastructure: trends, needs and the role of aid. *Habitat International*, **12**, 3, 139 - 147.

COTTON Andrew and FRANCEYS Richard, 1991. *Services for shelter*. Liverpool University Press, Liverpool.

COTTON Andrew, 1993. *Cuttack Slum Improvement Project: Infrastructure provision in the pilot slums.* Water, Engineering & Development Centre, Loughborough University of Technology.

COTTON Andrew, FRANCEYS Richard, PICKFORD John and SAYWELL Darren 1995 *On-plot sanitation in low income urban communities: a review of literature* WEDC, Loughborough University.

COTTON Andrew, 1997 *Appropriate sanitation options: Project No: WELL 18*, WELL, London

CHADHA Skylark and STRAUSS Martin, 1991. *Promotion of rural sanitation in Bangladesh with private sector participation.* Swiss Development Corporation, Dhaka, Bangladesh.

CROSS Piers, 1985. Existing practices and beliefs in the use of human excreta. *IRCWD News*, No 23, December, 2 - 4.

CURTIS Chris, 1982. Insect traps for pit latrines. *Appropriate technology*, **9**, 2, September, 11.

CURTIS Chris, 1991. New ideas in the control of mosquitoes. *Footsteps*, No 9, December, 10 - 11.

CURTIS C F and FEACHEM R G, 1981. Sanitation and *Culex pipiens* mosquitoes: a brief review. *Journal of Tropical Medicine and Hygiene*, **84**, 17 - 25.

CURTIS C F and HAWKINS P M, 1982, Entomological studies of on-site sanitation systems in Botswana and Tanzania. *Trans Royal Society of Tropical Medicine and Hygiene*, **76**, 1, February, 99 - 108.

CURTIS Donald, 1978. Values of latrine users and administrators. In *Sanitation in developing countries.* (Ed Pacey). John Wiley & Sons, Chichester. Pages 170 - 176.

DANISH INTERNATIONAL DEVELOPMENT AGENCY (DANIDA), 1991. *Village sanitation: survey of 629 households carried out in Matale District during April 1991*. Report No A21. Support to the rural water supply and sanitation sector in Matale, Polonnaruwa and Anuradhapura Districts for the National Water Supply and Drainage Board, Sri Lanka. Kampsax-Kruger, Copenhagen.

DE LEEUW C P, 1981. water supply and sewage disposal - experience in remote areas of Southern Africa. In *Appropriate technology in civil engineering*. Institution of Civil Engineers, London. Pages 43 - 45.

DEWIT Michael and SCHENK Hans, 1989. *Shelter for the poor in India: issues in low cost housing*. Manohar Publications, New Delhi.

DRAKAKIS-SMITH David, 1987. *The Third World city*. Routledge, London.

DREWRY WA and ELIASSEN R, 1968 Virus movement in groundwater. *J. Water Pollut.Control Fed.* **40** R257-R271

DUQUEHIN F L, 1978. *Personal communication*. (Now Jersey, Channel Islands; Kenya, early 1950s).

DWYER, D J. 1975. *People and housing in Third World cities*. Longman, London.

ENVIRONMENTAL HEALTH PROJECT 1997 *Better sanitation programming: a UNICEF handbook*. EHP Applied Study No. 5, Washington DC

ENVIRONMENTAL HEALTH PROJECT 1997 *Designing a sanitation programme for the urban poor: case study from Montego Bay, Jamaica*. Activity Report No. 34, EHP, Washington DC

ENVIRONMENTAL HEALTH PROJECT 1997 *Evaluation of the Jamaica urban environmental program for on-site sanitation*. Activity Report No. 35, EHP, Washington DC

EL-KATSHA Samiha, YOUNIS Awatif, EL-SEBAIE Olfat and HUSSEIN Ahmed (El-Katsha et al), 1989. *Women, water and sanitation: household water use in two Egyptian villages.* The American University in Cairo Press, Cairo.

ELMENDORF Mary and BUCKLES Patricia, 1980. Sociocultural aspects of water supply and excreta disposal. Appropriate technology for water supply and sanitation, volume 5. The World Bank, Washington DC.
ENFO, 1992. Promotion of rural sanitation in Egypt. *Enfo*, **14**, 1, March, page 12.

ESRAY Steven A, COLLETT Jim, Miliotis Marianne D, KOORNHOF Hendrick A and MAKHALE (Esray et al), 1989. The risk of infection from *Giardia lamblia* due to drinking water and latrines among preschool children in rural Lesotho. *International J Epidemiology*, **18**, 1, 248 - 253.

ESRAY S A, FEACHEM R G and HUGHES J M (Esrey et al), 1985. Interventions for the control of diarrhoeal diseases among young children: improving water supplies and excreta disposal facilities. *Bulletin of the World Health Organization*, **63**, 4, 757-772.

ESRAY Steven A, POTASH James B, ROBERTS Leslie and SHIFF Clive (Esray et al), 1990. *Health benefits from improvements in water supply and sanitation: survey and analysis of the literature on selected diseases.* WASH Technical Report No 66. WASH, Arlington, Va, USA.

FEACHEM R, BRADLEY D, GARELICK H and MARA D (Feachem et al), 1983(a). *Sanitation and disease: health aspects of excreta and wastewater management.* John Wiley and Sons, Chichester.

FEACHEM Richard G, GUY Malcolm W, HARRISON Shirley, IWUGO Kenneth O, MARSHALL Thomas, MBERE Nomtuse, MULLER Ralph and WRIGHT Albert M (Feachem et al), 1983(b). Excreta disposal facilities and intestinal parasitism in urban Africa: preliminary studies in Botswana, Ghana and Zambia. *Trans Royal Society of Tropical Medicine and Hygiene*, **77**, 4, 515 - 521.

FEACHEM R G, MARA D D and IWUGO K O (Feachem et al), 1978. *Alternative sanitation technologies for the urban poor in Africa*. Energy, Water and Telecommunications Department, The World Bank, Washington DC.

FEKPE et al, 1992 Percolation testing and soil evaluation for waste water treatment. *Proc. Inst. Civ. Eng. - Munic. Eng.* **93** 93-99

FLANAGAN Donna, 1988. *Human resources development in water and sanitation programmes: case studies from Togo, Sri Lanka, Philippines, Zaire and Thailand*. Training Series No 3. IRC, International Water and Sanitation Centre, The Hague.

FORMAN David, 1987. Gastric cancer, diet and nitrate exposure, *British Medical Journal*, 28 February, 294, 528 - 529.

FOURIE AB and van RYNEVELD MB 1995 The fate in the subsurface of contaminants associated with on-site sanitation: a review, *Water SA*, **21**, 2, April, 101-111.

FRANCEYS Richard, 1986. Dry latrines. Technical brief No 9. *Waterlines*, **5**, 1, July, 15 - 18.

FRANCEYS Richard, 1990. Guide to sanitation selection. *Waterlines*, **8**, 3, January, 15 - 18. Also in *The worth of water; technical briefs on health, water and sanitation*. Intermediate Technology Publications, London. Pages 93 - 96.

FRANCEYS Richard and COTTON Andrew, 1988. Services by a support approach: infrastructure for urban housing in Sri Lanka. *Open House International*, **13**, 4, 43 - 48.

FRANCEYS, R., PICKFORD, J., REED, R. 1992. *A Guide to the Development of On-Site Sanitation*. World Health Organisation, Geneva, Switzerland. ISBN 92 4 154443 0.

GEARHEART Robert A, 1991. *Ghana rural water project start-up workshop: World Vision and Hilton Foundation: January 7-10, 1991*. WASH Field Report No 345. WASH, Arlington, Va.

GERBA et al 1975 Fate of wastewater bacteria and viruses in soil. *J. Irrig. Drain. Div. ASCE.* **101** 157-174

GIBBS Ken, 1984. Privacy and the pit privy: technology or technique. *Waterlines*, **3**, 1, July, 19-21

GOVERNMENT OF INDIA (GOI), 1990. *People, water and sanitation: what they know, believe and do in rural India.* National Drinking Water Mission. GOI, New Delhi.

GLENSVIG Leo and GLENSVIG Dorte, 1989. Pour-flush toilets and waste stabilization ponds in a refugee camp. *Waterlines,* **8**, 1, July, 2 - 4.

GOLLADAY Fredrick L, 1983. *Meeting the needs of the poor for water supply and waste disposal.* A World Bank Technical Paper. The World Bank, Washington DC.

GOYDER Catherine, 1978. Voluntary and government sanitation programmes. In *Sanitation in developing countries* (Ed Pacey). John Wiley & Sons, Chichester. Pages 162 - 167.

GUPTA Rajiv, 1983. Are community biogas plants a feasible proposition? *World Health Forum*, **4**, 4, 358 - 361.

HAMMAR, A. and JUNIOR, B. 1994 *Sustainability of the national programme for low cost sanitation in Mozambique* HABITAT/UNCHS and UNDP, Maputo

HARDOY Jorge E, CAIRNCROSS Sandy and SATTERTHWAITE David (Hardoy et al), 1990. *The poor die young: housing and health in Third World cities.* Earthscan Publications, London.

HARPHAM Trudy, LUSTY Tim and VAUGHAN Patrick (Harpham et al), 1988. *In the shadow of the city: community health and the urban poor.* Oxford University Press, Oxford.

HARRIS R B, MASKELL A D, NJAU F Z and PICKFORD John *(Harris et al),* 1981. Dar-es-Salaam sewerage and sanitation study. In *Appropriate technology in civil engineering.* Institution of Civil Engineers, London. Pages 67-69

HARRISON Paul, 1987. *The greening of Africa: breaking through in the battle for land and food*. Grafton Books, London.

HINDHAUGH G M A, 1973. Night-soil treatment. *The Consulting Engineer*, September, 47, 49.

HOGREWE, W., JOYCE, S, and PEREZ, E., *The Unique Challenges of Peri-Urban Sanitation* WASH Technical Report No. 86, USAID, July 1993

HOPCRAFT Arthur, 1968. *Born to hunger*. Pan Books, London.

HOQUE Bilqis A, HOQUE M M, ALI, N and COGHLAN Sarah E, 1994. Sanitation in a poor settlement in Bangladesh: a challenge for the 1990s. *Environment and Urbanization*, **6**, 2, October, 79-85

HOWARTH D A, 1983. The role of development banks in international funding. In *Water supply and sanitation in developing countries* (Ed Dangerfield). Water Practice Manuals, Volume 3. The Institution of Water Engineers and Scientists. Pages 47 - 63.

HUBLEY John, 1987. Communication and health education planning for sanitation programmes. *Waterlines*, **5**, 3, January, 2 - 5.

HUNT Steven, 1986. Lucrative latrines. *IDRC Reports*, **15**, 4, October, page 13.

INTERNATIONAL DEVELOPMENT RESEARCH CENTRE, 1983. *The latrine project, Mozambique*. IDRC-MR58e. IDRC, Ottawa. (Brandberg,1983).

ISELEY Raymond B, FAIIA Scott, ASHWORTH John, DONOVAN Richard and THOMSON James (Iseley et al), 1986. *Framework and guidelines for Care water supply and sanitation projects*. WASH Technical Report No 40. WASH, Arlington, Va.

IWUGO Kenneth O, MARA D Duncan and FEACHEM Richard G (Iwugo et al), 1978a. *Sanitation studies in Africa*. A research study of the World Bank. Sanitation Site Report Number 1, Ibadan, Nigeria. The World Bank, New York.

IWUGO Kenneth O, MARA D Duncan and FEACHEM Richard G (Iwugo et al), 1978b. *Sanitation studies in Africa*. A research study of the World Bank. Sanitation Site Report Number 4, Zambia (Lusaka and Ndola). The World Bank, New York.

JEEYASEELEN S, LOHANI B N and VIRARAGHAVAN T (Jeeyaseelen et al), 1987. *Low-cost rural sanitation - problems and solutions*. ENSIC, Bangkok.

JOINT COMMITTEE ON MEDICAL ASPECTS OF WATER QUALITY (Joint Committee), 1984. *Advice on nitrate in drinking water in relation to a suggested cancer risk*. Department of Health and Social Security/Department of the Environment. HMSO, London.

KALBERMATTEN J M, JULIUS D S and GUNNERSON C G (Kalbermatten et al), 1982(a). *Appropriate sanitation alternatives: a technical and economic appraisal*. World Bank studies in water supply and sanitation 1. John Hopkins University Press, Baltimore.

KALBERMATTEN John M, 1991. Water and sanitation for all, will it become reality or remain a dream? *Water International*, **16**, 3, September, 121 - 126.

KAOMA J, 1981. Zambia's experience with aqua-privies. In *Sanitation in developing countries*. Proceedings of a workshop on training held in Lobatse, Botswana, 14-20 August 1980. IDRC, Ottawa. Pages 41 - 47.

KILAMA W and MINJAS J, 1985. The mounting Culex p. quinquefasciatus problem in urban East Africa. In *Water and sanitation in Africa*. Proc 11th WEDC Conference, Dar es Salaam, April 1985. WEDC, Loughborough.

KINLEY David, 1992. Kumasi's people for better sanitation services. *Source*, **4**, 1, July, 4 - 9.

KOTALOVA J, 1984. *Personal and domestic hygiene in rural Bangladesh*. SIDA, Stockholm.

LACEY Linda and OWUSU Steven E, 1988. Squatter settlements in Monrovia, Liberia: the evolution of housing policies. In *Slum and squatter settlements in Sub-Saharan Africa: toward a planning strategy* (Ed. Obudho and Mhlanga). Praeger, New York.

LAGERSTEDT E., JACKS G. and SEFE F 1994 Nitrate in groundwater and N circulation in eastern Botswana *Environmental Geology*, **23**, 1, 60-64
LAVER Sue, 1986. Communications for low-cost sanitation in Zimbabwe. *Waterlines*, **4**, 4, April, 26 - 28.

LAVER Sue, 1988. Learning to share knowledge - a Zimbabwean case study. *Waterlines*, **6**, 3, January, 6 - 8.

LAWLESS Richard I and FINDLEY Allan M, 1981. Tunis. In *Problems and planning in Third World cities* (Ed Pacione). Pages 94 - 126.

LEA John P and COURTNEY John M (Ed), 1985. *Cities in conflict: studies in the planning and management of Asian cities*. World Bank, Washington, DC.

LEWIS W John, FOSTER Stephen S D and DRASAR Bohumil S (Lewis et al), 1982. *The risk of groundwater pollution by on-site sanitation in developing countries - a literature review*. IRCWD Report No 01/82. International Reference Centre for Wastes Disposal, Duebendorf, Switzerland.

LOCHERY Peter W S and ADU-ASAH Seth T, no date. *Building and operating multi-compartment VIP latrines*. Lagos, Nigeria.

LOHANI Kumar and GUHR Ingo, 1985. *Alternative sanitation in Bhaktapur, Nepal: an exercise in community participation*. GTZ, Eschborn.

LOWDER Stella, 1986. *Inside Third World Cities*. Croom & Helm, London.

McAUSLAN Patrick, 1985. *Urban land and shelter for the poor*. Earthscan, London.

McCOMMON Carolyn, WARNER Dennis and YOHALEM David (McCommon et al), 1990. *Community management of rural water supply and sanitation services.* UNDP-World Bank Water and Sanitation Program Discussion Paper Series, DP Number 4. World Bank, Washington, DC.

McMICHAEL Joan K, 1978. The double septic bin in Vietnam. In *Sanitation in developing countries* (Ed Pacey). John Wiley & Sons, Chichester. Pages 110 - 114.

MAI Sanan Na Chiang and KUKIELKA Boleslaw Jan, 1981. *Review of experiences with self-help family latrine project at Ban Khuan of Hang Chat District and possible application of these experiences in environmental health project.* Ref No N/55/27. Ministry of Public Health, Bangkok.

MAITRA M S, 1978. Sanitation for the urban poor in Calcutta. In *Sanitation in developing countries* (Ed Pacey). Wiley, Chichester. Pages 144 - 152.

MARA D Duncan, 1984. *The design of ventilated improved pit latrines.* TAG Technical Note No 13. The World Bank, Washington DC.

MARA Duncan, 1985. *Ventilated improved pit latrines: guidelines for the selection of design options.* TAG Discussion Paper No 4. The World Bank, Washington DC.

MARA D D and SINNATAMBY G S, 1986. Rational design of septic tanks in warm climates. *Public Health Engineer*, **14**, 4, 49 - 55.

MARA Duncan, 1996 *Low cost urban sanitation* John Wiley & Sons, Chichester

MARAIS G v R, 1973. Sanitation and low cost housing. In *Water quality: management and pollution control problems* (Ed. Jenkins). Pergamon, Oxford. Pages 115 - 125.

MATHÉY Koste (Ed), 1991. *Beyond self-help housing.* Mansell Publishing, London.

MITRA H N, 1990. Housing and health in three squatter settlements in Allahabad, India. In *The poor die young* (Ed Hardoy et al). Earthscan Publications, London. Pages 89 - 108.

MOES W and ZWAGG R R, 1984. Low cost solutions often beat sewers. *World Water*, September, 56 - 57.

MOHANRAO G J, 1973. Waste water and refuse treatment and disposal in India. In *Environmental health engineering in hot climates and developing countries* (Ed Pickford). WEDC, Loughborough. Pages 69 - 86.

MORGAN Peter, 1977. The pit latrine - revived. *Central African J Medicine*, **23**, 1 - 4.

MORGAN Peter, 1990. *Rural water supplies and sanitation: a text from Zimbabwe's Blair Resarch Laboratory*. Macmillan, Basingstoke.

MORGAN Peter R and MARA D Duncan, 1982. *Ventilated improved pit latrines: recent developments in Zimbabwe*. World Bank Technical Paper No 3. The World Bank, Washington DC.

MORLEY David, ROHDE Jon and WILLIAMS Glen (Ed), 1983. *Practising health for all*. Oxford University Press, Oxford.

MORROW Richard H, 1983. A primary health care strategy for Ghana. In *Practising health for all* (Ed Morley, Rohde and Williams). Oxford University Press, Oxford. Pages 272 - 299.

MOSER Caroline O N, 1991. Women and self-help housing projects: a conceptual framework for analysis and policy-making. In *Beyond self-help housing* (Ed Mathéy). Mansell Publishing, London. Pages 53 - 73.

MOSER Caroline O N and PEAKE Linda, 1987. Women, human settlements, and housing. Tavistock Publications, London.

MOWFORTH K and AGGARWAL K K, 1985. Development of the Buguruni-type VIP. In Water and sanitation in Africa. Proc 11th WEDC Conference, Dar es Salaam, 15 - 19 April 1985. WEDC, Loughborough.

MULLICK M A, 1987. *Socio-economic aspects of rural water supply and sanitation: a case study of the Yemen Arab Republic*. The Book Guild, Lewes, Sussex.

MULLER, M. 1991. *Institutional arrangements for low cost sanitation in Mozambique: study and draft proposals.* Swiss Development Cooperation, Berne

NARAYAN-PARKER Deepa, 1989. *Goals and indicators for integrated water supply and sanitation projects in partnership with people.* PROWWESS/UNDP Technical Series. PROWESS/UNDP, New York.

NJAU Frederick Z, 1981. Sewerage and low-cost sanitation: a solution to sanitation problems in developing countries. In *Sanitation in developing countries.* Proceedings of a workshop on training held in Lobatse, Botswana, 14-20 August 1980. IDRC, Ottawa. Pages 56 - 58.

NOSTRAND John van and WILSON James G, 1983. *The ventilated improved double-pit latrine: a construction manual for Botswana.* TAG Technical Note No 3. The World Bank, Washington DC.

OBUDHO R A and MHLANGA Constance C (Ed), 1988. *Slum and squatter settlements in Sub-Saharan Africa: towards a planning strategy.* Praeger, New York.

OENDO A, 1983. *Sanitation, health and the community in Kibwezi.* AMREF, Nairobi

OTIS R, 1983. *Small diameter gravity sewers: an alternative wastewater collection method for unsewered communities.* Report prepared for the United States Environmental Protection Agency (USEPA). Municipal Environmental Research Laboratory, Office of Research and Development, USEPA, Cincinnati, USA.

OTIS R J and MARA D D, 1985. *The design of small bore sewer systems.* TAG Technical Note No 14. The World Bank, Washington, DC.

PACIONE Michael, 1981 (Ed). *Problems and planning in Third World cities.* Croom Helm, London.

PARLATO Ronald, 1984. *A monitoring and evaluation manual for low-cost sanitation programs in India.* TAG Technical Note No 12. The World Bank, Washington DC.

PASHA Hafiz A and Michael G McGarry (*Editors*), 1989. *Rural water supply and sanitation in Pakistan.*World Bank Technical Paper Number 105. The World Bank, Washington, DC.

PASTEUR D, 1979. The Ibadan comfort stations programme: a case-study of the community development approach to environmental health improvement. *Journal of Administration Overseas*, **18**, 1, 46 - 58.

PAWLOWSKI Z S, 1985. Ascariasis control. *World Health Forum*, **6**, 3, 254-256.

PEEL C, 1967. The problem of excremental disease in tropical Africa. *Journal of Tropical Medicine and Hygiene*, **70**, June, 141 - 152.

PESCOD M B, 1983. Low-cost technology. In *Water practice manuals. Volume 3: Water supply and sanitation in developing countries* (Ed Dangerfield). Pages 263 - 295.

PICKFORD John, 1977. *Indexed bibliography of publications on water and waste engineering for developing countries.* WEDC, Loughborough.

PICKFORD John, 1980. *The design of septic tanks and aqua-privies.* BRE Overseas Building Notes. No 187, September. Overseas Division, Building Research Establishment, Gartree.

PICKFORD John, 1984(a). Good hardware + appropriate software = successful implementation. *Waterlines*, **2**, 3, January, 2 - 4.

PICKFORD John, 1984(b). Training people to meet the global need. In *Water and sanitation: economic and sociological perspectives* (Ed Bourne). Academic Press, Orlando. Pages 199 - 219.

PICKFORD John, 1987. Waste disposal technology for households without piped water. *Trib Cebedeau* (Belgium), No 519, 41 - 48.

PICKFORD John, 1988. Sewerage. Technical Brief No 10. *Waterlines*, **6**, 4, April, 15 - 18. Also in *The worth of water: technical briefs on health, water and sanitation.* Intermediate Technology Publications, London, 1991. Pages 65 - 68.

PICKFORD John, 1990(a). Urgent urban water and waste problems. *Waterlines*, **9**, 1, July, 2 - 5.

PICKFORD John, 1990(b). Community and infrastructure in some Asian cities. In *Planning, shelter and services*. Proc 7th Inter-Schools Conference. WEDC, Loughborough. Pages 61 - 66.

PICKFORD John, 1991a. Public and communal latrines. Technical Brief No 28. *Waterlines* , **9**, 3, 15 - 19. Also in *The worth of water*. IT Publications, London, 1991. Pages 113 - 116.

PICKFORD John, 1992. Latrine vent pipes. Technical Brief No 31. *Waterlines*, **10**, 3, January, 15 - 18. Also in *The worth of water: technical briefs on health, water and sanitation*. Intermediate Technology Publications, London, 1991. Pages 125 - 128.

PICKFORD John, 1995 *Low cost sanitation: a survey of practical experience* Intermediate Technology Publications, London

PROUDFOOT David and NARE Lerato, 1996 *Impact study of the national programme for low cost sanitation in Mozambique* Institute of Water and Sanitation Development, Zimbabwe

RAHMAN Mizanur, RAHAMAN M Mujibur, WOJTYNIAK Bogdan and AZIZ K M S (Rahman et al), 1985. Impact of environmental sanitation and crowding on infant mortality in rural Bangladesh. *The Lancet*, 6 July, ii, 28 - 31.

RAJESWARY I, 1992. Mahalapye's latrines sink no more. *Source*, **4**, 1, July, 10 - 13.

REED Bob and VINES Marcus, 1989. Reduced cost sewerage - does it work? In *Water, engineering and development in Africa*. Proceedings of the 15th WEDC Conference, Kano, Nigeria, 3 - 7 April 1989. WEDC, Loughborough. Pages 111 - 114.

REMEDIOS A P, 1981. Ecological balance in Goa. In *Appropriate technology in civil engineering*. Institution of Civil Engineers, London. Pages 46 - 48.

RIBEIRO Edgar F, 1985. *Improved sanitation and environmental health conditions: an evaluation of Sulabh International's low cost sanitation project in Bihar*. Sulabh International, Patna.

RIJNSBURGER Jaap, 1991. Emptying pit latrines: WASTE fills a vacuum in Dar es Salaam, Tanzania. *AT Source*, **18**, 2, 29 - 33.

ROBERTS Martin, 1987. Sewage collection and disposal. In *Affordable housing projects: a training manual: Readings*. Prepared for the United Nations Centre for Human Settlements (Habitat). Development Planning Unit, London.

ROBSON Emma, 1991. China's centuries-old recycling tradition gears for the future. *Source*, **3**, 4, December, 5 - 11.

ROMERO JC 1972 The movement of bacteria and viruses through porous media. In: Pettyjohn, W A (ed) *Water Quality in a Stressed Environment*. Burgess Publishing Company, Minnesota, 200-224.

ROSENHALL L, 1990. Water supply and sanitation in rural Burma - towards convergence. *Water Quality Bulletin*, **15**, 1, January, 46 - 51, 64, 65.

ROY A K, CHATTERJEE P K, GUPTA K N, KHARE S T, RAU B B and SINGH R S (Roy et al), 1984 *Manual on the design, construction and maintenance of low-cost pour-flush waterseal latrines in India*. TAG Technical Note Number 10. The World Bank, Washington DC.

RYAN Beverley A and MARA D Duncan, 1983. *Ventilated improved pit latrines: vent pipe design guidelines*. TAG Technical Note No 6. The World Bank, Washington DC.

RYBCZYNSKI Witold, POLPRASERT Chongrak and McGARRY Michael, 1978. *Low-cost technical options for sanitation: a state-of-the-art review and annotated bibliography*. IDRC-102e. IDRC, Ottawa.

SAGAR Gyan, 1983. A dwarf septic tank developed in India. *Waterlines*, **2**, 1, July, 22 - 23.

SCHERTENLEIB Roland and HAWKINS Peter, 1983. *Problems related to emptying on-site excreta disposal systems.* Paper presented at the International Seminar on Human Waste Management for Low Income Settlements, Bangkok, 16 - 22 January 1983.

SENGUPTA C, 1996. Pollution travel from leach pits. In *Reaching the Unreached: Challenges for the C21st.* Proceedings 22nd WEDC Conference, New Delhi, September 1996. WEDC, Loughborough.

SHUVAL Hillel I, ADIN Avner, FATTAL Badri, RAWITZ Eliyahu and YEKUTIEL (Shuval et al), 1986. *Wastewater irrigation in developing countries: health effects and technical solutions.* World Bank Technical Paper Number 51. The World Bank, Washington DC.

SHUVAL Hillel I, GUNNERSON Charles G and JULIUS DeAnne S (Shuval et al), 1981. *Night-soil composting.* The World Bank, Washington DC.

SHUVAL H I, YEKUTIEL P and FATTAL B (Shuval et al), 1984. Epidemiological evidence for helminth and cholera transmission by vegetables irrigated with wastewater: Jerusalem - a case study. *Water Science and Technology*, **17**, 433 - 442.

SILVA Kalinga Tudor and ATHUKORALA Karunatissa, 1991. *The watta-dwellers: a sociological study of selected urban low-income communities in Sri Lanka.* University Press of America, Lanham.

SIMPSON-HEBERT Mayling, 1984. Water and sanitation: cultural considerations. In *Water and sanitation: economic and sociological perspectives* (Ed Bourne). Academic Press, Orlando. Pages 174 - 198.

SINHA Bakshi D and GHOSH Arun K, 1990. *Evaluation of low-cost sanitation: liberation, training and rehabilitation of scavengers.* Arnold Publishers, New Delhi.

SINNATAMBY Gehan, 1990. Low cost sanitation. In *The poor die young* (Ed Hardoy et al). Earthscan Publications, London. Pages 127 - 157.

SINNATAMBY G, MARA D and McGARRY M (Sinnatamby et al), 1986. Shallow systems offer hope to slums. *World Water*, 9, No 1, 39-41.

SKODA John D, MENDIS J Bertrand and CHIA Michael (Skoda et al), 1978. The impact of sanitation in Bangladesh. In *Sanitation in developing countries* (Ed Pacey). John Wiley & Sons, Chichester. Pages 33 - 34.

SOTO Harnando de, 1989. *The other path: the invisible revolution in the Third World.* Tauris, London.

SRIDHAR M K C and OMISHAKIN M A, 1985. An evaluation of the water supply and sanitation problems in Nigeria. *Journal of the Royal Society of Health*, **105**, 2, 68 - 72.

STRAUSS Martin, 1985. Health aspects of nightsoil and sludge use in agriculture and aquaculture: Part II:Survival of excreted pathogens in excreta and faecal sludges. *IRCWD News*, No 23, 49.

STRUYK Raymond, 1989. *Assessing housing needs and policy alternatives in developing countries.* Urban Institute Report 88-4. University Press of America.

SUBRAMANIUM S K, 1978. Biogas systems and sanitation. In *Sanitation in developing countries*. (Ed Pacey). John Wiley & Sons, Chichester. Pages 191 - 194.

TAUSSIG DM and CONNELLY RJ, 1991 Investigation into the Nitrate Contamination of Groundwater in Kutama and Sinthumule Districts, Venda. SRK (CE) Inc. Report #164234/1

THOLIN A L, 1971. The evolution of a master plan. In *Water supply and wastewater disposal in developing countries* (Ed Pescod and Okum). AIT, Bangkok. Pages 70 - 78.

TIM US and MOSTAGHIMI S, 1991 Model for predicting virus movement through soils. *Ground Water* **29** (2) 251-259.
TOBIN V, 1985. Sanitation training in Nepal. *Waterlines*, **4**, 2, October, 13 - 15.

TRAINER Edward S, 1985. Mass parasite control: a new beginning. *World Health Forum*, **6**, 3, 248-253.

TRUNEH Aragaw, 1981. Sanitary situation in Addis Ababa. In *Sanitation in developing countries*. Proceedings of a workshop on training held in Lobatse, Botswana, 14-20 August 1980. IDRC, Ottawa. Pages 52 - 55.

UNDP-WORLD BANK WATER AND SANITATION PROGRAM and PROWESS (UNDP-World Bank), 1990. *Rural sanitation in Lesotho: from pilot project to national program*. The World Bank, Washington DC.

UNDP-WORLD BANK WATER AND SANITATION PROGRAM - RWSG-WA 1994. *Ouagadougou and Kumasi sanitation projects: a comparative case study* The World Bank

UNDP-WORLD BANK WATER AND SANITATION PROGRAM - RWSG-SA 1997. *Regional workshop on sanitation for low income urban communities: proceedings, February 1997*. The World Bank, New Delhi.

UNICEF, 1991. *The state of the world's children 1991*. OUP, Oxford.

UNICEF, 1992. *The state of the world's children 1992*. OUP, Oxford.

UNITED NATIONS, 1990. *Report A/45/327 of the Secretary General of the Economic and Social Council to the UN General Assembly*. July 1990. United Nations, New York.

UNITED NATIONS CENTRE FOR HUMAN SETTLEMENTS (UNCHS), 1980. *Physical improvement of slums and squatter settlements*. Report of an Ad Hoc Expert Group Meeting held in Nassau, 31 January - 4 February 1977. CHS/R/80-1/S. UNCHS, Nairobi.

UNITED NATIONS CENTRE FOR HUMAN SETTLEMENTS (UNCHS), 1982. *Appropriate infrastructure services, standards and technology*. Report of the *ad hoc* expert working group meeting on appropriate services, standards and technologies for upgrading slums and squatter areas and rural settlements. Nairobi, 2 - 9 November 1981. HS/OP/82-10. UNCHS, Nairobi.

UNITED NATIONS CENTRE FOR HUMAN SETTLEMENTS (UNCHS), 1984. *A review of technologies for the provision of basic infrastructure in low-income settlements*. HS/40/84/E. UNCHS, Nairobi.

UNITED NATIONS CENTRE FOR HUMAN SETTLEMENTS (UNCHS), 1986a. *Sociocultural perspective of sanitation in Nepal: a survey report.* UNCHS, Nairobi.

UNITED NATIONS CENTRE FOR HUMAN SETTLEMENTS (UNCHS), 1986b. *The design of shallow sewer systems.* UNCHS, Nairobi.

UNITED NATIONS CENTRE FOR HUMAN SETTLEMENTS (UNCHS), 1986c. *Community participation in low-cost sanitation - training module.* UNCHS, Nairobi.

UNITED NATIONS CENTRE FOR HUMAN SETTLEMENTS (UNCHS), 1989. *The maintenance of infrastructure and its financing and cost recovery.* UNCHS, Nairobi.

UNITED STATES ENVIRONMENTAL PROTECTION AGENCY (USEPA), 1984. *Handbook: Septage treatment and disposal.* EPA-625/6-84-009. USEPA, Cincinnati.

UNITED STATES ENVIRONMENTAL PROTECTION AGENCY (USEPA), 1987. *Design manual: dewatering municipal wastewater sludges.* EPA/625/1-87/014. USEPA, Cincinnati.

UNITED STATES ENVIRONMENTAL PROTECTION AGENCY (USEPA), 1991. *Manual: Alternative wastewater collection systems.* EPA/625/1-91/024. USEPA, Cincinnati.

UNRAU G O, 1978. Water seal pit latrines. In *Sanitation in developing countries*(Ed Pacey). John Wiley & Sons, Chichester. Pages 104 - 106.

URBAN EDGE The, 1987. India implements latrine program on a large scale. *The Urban Edge*, **11**, 10, December, 1 - 3.

VINES Marcus and REED Bob, 1990. Low-cost unconventional sewerage. *Waterlines*, **9**, 1, July, 26 - 29.

WAGNER E G and LANOIX J N, 1958. *Excreta disposal for rural areas and small communities.* World Health Organization, Geneva.

WANG L H and TAN T H, 1981. Singapore In *Problems and planning in Third World cities* (Ed Pacione). Croom Helm, London. Pages 218 - 249.

WATT Jim and LAING Richard O, 1985. Teaching aids for water and sanitation. *Waterlines*, **3**, 4, April, 25 - 27.

WEGELIN-SCHURINGA Madeleen, 1991. *On-site sanitation: building on local practice*. IRC, The Hague.

WHEELER D and CARROLL R F, 1989. The minimisation of microbiological hazards associated with latrine wastes. *Water Science and Technology*, **21**, 3, 35 - 42.

WHITE Alistair, 1981. *Community participation in water and sanitation: concepts, strategies and methods*. Technical Paper No 17. International Centre for Community Water Supply and Sanitation, The Hague.

WHITTINGTON Dale, Lauria Donald T, WRIGHT Albert M, CHOE Kyeongae, HUGHES Jeffrey A and SWARNA Venkateswarlu (Whittington et al), 1992. *Household demand for improved sanitation services: a case study of Kumasi, Ghana*. The World Bank, Washington DC.

WHYTE Anne V, 1984. Community participation: neither panacea nor myth. In *Water and sanitation: economic and sociological perspectives* (Ed Bourne). Academic Press, Orlando. Pages 221 - 241.

WIJK-SIJBESMA Christine van, 1979. *Participation and education in community water supply and sanitation programmes: a literature review*. Technical Paper 12. International Reference Centre for Community Water Supply and Sanitation, The Hague.

WIJK-SIJBESMA Christine van, 1985. *Participation of women in water supply and sanitation: roles and realities*. Technical Paper 22. International Reference Centre for Community Water Supply and Sanitation, The Hague.

WILLIAMS Chris, 1987. Choices in pit latrine emptying. In *Rural water and engineering development in Africa*. Proc 13th WEDC Conference, Lilongwe. WEDC, Loughborough. Pages 28 - 31.

WILLIAMSON J R, 1983. Towards community managed drinking water schemes in Nepal. *Waterlines*, **2**, 2, October, 8 - 13.

WINBLAD Uno, KILAMA Wen and TORSTENSSON K, 1985. *Sanitation without water*. Macmillan, Basingstoke.

WORLD HEALTH ORGANIZATION (WHO), 1982. *Benefits to health of safe and adequate drinking water and sanitary disposal of human waste: imperative considerations for the International Drinking Water Supply and Sanitation Decade*. EHE/82.32. WHO, Geneva.

WORLD HEALTH ORGANIZATION (WHO), 1987. *Evaluation of the strategy for health for all by the year 2000: Seventh report on the world health situation*. Volume 1, Global review. WHO, Geneva.

WORLD HEALTH ORGANIZATION (WHO), 1991. Surface water drainage for low-income communities. WHO, Geneva.

WORLD HEALTH ORGANISATION (1995a) *Community water supply and sanitation: needs challenges and health objectives*. Report by the Director-General to the Forty-Eighth World Health Assembly.

WORLD HEALTH ORGANISATION (1996 *Creating Healthy Cities in the 21st Century*. Geneva.

WORLD WATER, 1983. What is a pour-flush waterseal latrine? *World Water*, **6**, 12, December, p34.

WRIGHT A M, OWUSU S E and HANDA V K, 1978. Availability of latrines in a developing country. In *Sanitation in developing countries* (Ed. Pacey). Wiley, Chichester. Pages 4 - 10.

YOUNG B and BRISCOE J, 1987. *Water and health in rural Malawi: aspects of performance, utilization and health impact of the Malawi Self Help Rural Water Supply Project*. USAID, Washington DC.

ZACHER W, 1982. The significance of water and sanitation for primary health care workers in developing countries. *Internat J Hygiene Education*, **2**, 1, 21 -30.

ZAJAC Vincent, MERTODININGRAT Susanto, SUSANTO H Soewasti and LUDWIG Harvey F, *1984. Urban sanitation planning manual based on the Jakarta case study*. Technical Paper No 18. The World Bank, Washington DC.

Section 2E
Annex

Total Annual Cost per Household

An extension of the least cost analysis approach is to consider the total annual cost per household (TACH) (Kalbermatten et al, 1982). TACH is calculated by considering the total present value (PV) of the life-cycle cash flow as the equivalent of a loan which has to be paid back over the design life of the system at constant, non-inflated prices. The value of yearly repayments, including interest, is obtained by mulitiplying the present value by a capital recovery factor. This factor is taken from capital recovery factor tables which are based on the equation:

Capital recovery factor

$$= \frac{r(1 + r)^t}{(1 + r)^t - 1}$$

where

r = discount rate

t = design life in years